THE GUINEA KID

THE GUINEA KID

THE TRUE STORY
OF A CHILDHOOD CANCER SURVIVOR

By Sharon Ruth

North Grenville Press
Kemptville, ON K0G1J0 Canada
www.northgrenvillepress.com

©2008 Sharon Ruth

Published by North Grenville Press
in association with
Lunan Corporation
Kemptville, ON K0G1J0 Canada

www.northgrenvillepress.com

All rights reserved. Except as permitted under the Copyright Act, no part of this publication may be reproduced or distributed in any form or by any means, or stored in a database or retrieval system without the prior written permission of the publisher.

Cover photo courtesy Sun Media Corp.

Printed in the United States of America.

Library and Archives Canada Cataloguing in Publication

Ruth, Sharon, 1965-
    The guinea kid : the true story of a childhood cancer survivor / by Sharon Ruth.

ISBN 978-1-894966-01-6 (pbk.)

1. Ruth, Colleen. 2. Cancer in children--Patients--Canada--Biography. 3. Cancer--Patients--Canada--Biography. 4. Sick children--Canada--Biography. I. Title.

RC281.C4R88 2008   362.198'929940092   C2008-902836-8

Dedication

This book is the result of so many unexpected experiences. Not all of these were pleasant. You have a choice to accept the good with the bad, and get on with it. Or, you can take your dealt cards, and wallow in it.

I dedicate this book to my family and my friends, and some very caring people at the Children's Hospital of Eastern Ontario. Without your encouragement and support I could never have had the energy to re-live and write about the last few years, without falling endlessly into the wallow.

> A sense of purpose can breed passion.
> With passion you seek change.
> With change you get progress,
> Where new ideas can take full reign.

About the Author

Sharon Ruth is a mother of three (Ella, Ryan and Colleen) and wife of one (Danny). An Ontario Scholar, she was the recipient of the Chancellor's Scholarship to McMaster University and holds a degree in Sociology and a diploma in Personal Financial Planning.

Sharon lost both parents and a sister to cancer. Sharon lives with her family near Oxford Station in Ontario and fights for the rights of those families coping with this disease.

Preface

    The bag read BIOHAZARD and was filled with a sickly brown liquid. The yellow skull and crossbones that stretched across the plastic fluid seemed to look directly at me as if testing my resolve and patience to the fullest.

    She put on a mask and a gown and protective gloves before handling it. I sat and watched as she carefully attached it with tubing and a large sharp needle that could easily penetrate any material so its contents could flow freely when she opened the valve.

    Slowly, carefully, painstakingly, she prepared the surface that needed to be cleansed and sterile to ensure the toxic formula could be effective in its mission.

    I held my breath at the same time as the nurse inserted the needle into my six-year-old daughter's waiting arm and wondered what I was allowing to happen to my child?

    Seconds after the valve was opened , there was no turning back as the chemo poured freely into her bloodstream, and the reality came crushing down with tremendous force that I had no idea what would happen to her, no one did, and they had no idea what would remain of her when the treatments were over….

    I opened my eyes and gasped for breath all at the same time. My eyes stung from the salty sweat dripping from my forehead. I could barely catch my breath and my heart was racing so fast I felt it might explode from my chest. I looked over at my husband sleeping peacefully and longed to be able to be rid of the nightmares that besieged my sleep each night and kept me awake for hours long after they are passed.

    Another nightmare, that was all. Everything was fine. I turned onto my back and tried to drift off into sleep. It was no use. I was up for awhile. As I contemplated whether I would stay in bed, or get up and read or watch TV, I heard a small gasp for breath from the other room. I bolted from bed and decided to check on the children.

    I checked my son's room first. He was sleeping peacefully all tangled up in his blankets and the dog was on the floor beside his bed. Everything looked fine here.

    The girls shared a room. My oldest was completely covered by her duvet and I had to pull a corner down to make sure she was still breathing. She stirred as I disturbed her sleep but she settled down again very quickly pulling the covers back over her head and turning over in the bed.

    There was a chill in the air and I couldn't blame her for covering up. The room had needed a new window and some insulation over three years ago, but some unexpected financial complications came up and we had to put our plans on hold. Maybe some day soon we would get back on track.

    My youngest daughter, now 10, was also sleeping soundly in a bed on the other side of the room. Unlike her sister Ella, she had kicked off all her covers and I could see a fine line of perspiration on her upper lip. I put my hand to her forehead to feel if she was feverish. She felt a little warm, and her cheeks were rosy, but I didn't think she had a fever. She seemed to be breathing hard and I could tell she too was in the middle of a dream. The sound must have come from her.

I remembered my nightmare as I tried to cover her up with the blankets tangled in her feet at the bottom of the bed and hoped she was having a good dream. Mine wasn't a nightmare after all. I was remembering what had happened over three years ago. My subconscious was working overtime these days and there always seemed to be a sinister quality to my dreams. I think I may have read one too many horror novels over the years.

As I silently retreated from the room back to bed satisfied that all my little ducklings were fine, I wondered when my nightmares would stop. In bed and staring at the numbers on the clock radio slowly turn over towards dawn, I wished with all my heart that I could go back in time. That just now in her room I could have looked down upon a healthy six-year-old little girl, still innocent, still untouched and still uninfected by the miracles of modern medicine.

As I think back over the last few years and the roller coaster we had no choice to ride, I still have no idea why this happened to us. I don't think we'll ever understand the reasons. There's no one to blame though. Some families blame God. Some families blame the environment. Some families blame genetics. Some people blame each other. Some people blame the government.

I don't want to waste my life trying to find someone to blame. It produces too much negative energy and time is precious and should be filled with joy and peace and happy thoughts.

I believe everything happens for a reason, and I struggle to find the reason for my daughter's illness everyday. I am writing this book because I am hoping that it might help some people, to applaud some silent heroes, and to enlighten the people that have the power to effect change. There is so much support but so much more that needs to be done.

So read on if you want a peek into a World so foreign and frightening that you'll forever be worried something so unexpected could happen to you. My hope is, that if you do find yourself at the mercy of modern medicine, then your path will be less rocky and your journey less worrisome.

Chapter One

In order to tell the story properly I need to go back to the beginning. Back to when things were normal. Back to when our main concerns were who was helping whom with homework, and did we have enough milk for dinner and snacks for lunch bags the next day.

March, 2003

I got a call from the school. Colleen was sick and running a temperature. I was at work and expecting some clients shortly. They couldn't reach my husband and so they called me. In a panic I managed to contact my clients and reschedule, cleared off my desk, and raced off wondering what it was this time.

It seemed that she was getting sick a lot lately. She had turned six in September and was halfway through Grade 1. She loved school so much and I knew she would be disappointed to be sent home. Colleen never complained and would actually downplay any illness just so she could stay at school. Unfortunately this time her fever was too high and no amount of acting could cover that up.

When I arrived at the school I went straight to the office. There she was sitting in a chair. She was wearing her little Barbie backpack and was all ready for me when I got there. I could tell she wasn't happy to be going home; apparently they were supposed to be doing some crafts in the afternoon which she really wanted to do.

"How are you feeling, Honey?" I asked putting my hand to her brow.

"I'm fine," she said trying to avoid my eyes.

Her forehead was extremely warm. She started to cough a little and her cheeks were very rosy. She was blowing her nose yet what was coming out was actually clear. I made a mental note that if she had an infection the discharge would be a different colour. She probably had caught the flu again, some virus that would pass in a few days. We had all got our flu shots in the fall. Wasn't that supposed to stop her from getting sick?

"Come on Honey, let's go home. Hopefully Daddy will be there because I really have to get back to work." I said wishing I could just take the rest of the day off and curl up in bed with her. But I knew I had more appointments booked so quickly dismissed the thought.

My husband was currently driving a school bus but was actively looking for full-time work. We had moved with my Company a few times over the years, and there was a slowdown in his field. The economy was strong now, and he was looking forward to getting back to what he was trained in and making more money.

Two days later as I was leaving for work I said to my husband, "She's still running a high fever; I'm starting to get worried that this is more than the flu."

"Some of the kids on my bus have been away for days, Sharon. It's probably just the flu." I hated it when he sounded so sure and I was feeling uneasy.

"Still, I'm going to call the doctor anyway and make an appointment. I just want to be sure."

The doctor told us that she had the flu virus that was everywhere in Town. He prescribed plenty of fluids and Tylenol for her temperature. Feeling relieved with his diagnosis and trusting unquestionably in his abilities we headed home past a cramped waiting room with other children and adults who appeared to be suffering from the same thing.

I wondered when I, or the other kids, would come down with it next? I felt a little foolish for overreacting when it was obvious that she only had a virus. Next time I would try to be a little more patient before wasting the doctor's time and taking up someone else's much-needed appointment.

April, 2003

Easter was going to be early this year. We had invited my husband's entire family who lived out of town as well as my sister and her daughter. My sister's husband was not living with her anymore so we didn't need to worry about him. Their separation didn't come as a surprise to me considering the things I had seen over the years; however I respected her choices and kept my mouth shut during their 20 years of marriage.

"I'm looking forward to seeing you soon, Mom." I said to my mother-in-law wondering which bed I could give her that would be good for her back. "Don't worry, the kids are all sleeping on the floor, the adults all get beds."

After a couple of more minutes I said goodbye and hung up the phone. I was at work and my message light was blinking. The blink had a different look about it. My imagination got the best of me and it looked like an evil red eye flashing insistently and knowingly at me. I felt a terrible sense of dread and had to force myself to retrieve the call.

I picked up the phone and punched in my password to retrieve the message.

"Mrs. Ruth, its Marilyn at Holy Cross calling. We tried to reach your husband but there's no answer at home. Colleen's sick again and we need you to come get her when you get this message."

Great! I thought. Easter was just around the corner and it had been no more than a week or two since the last flu virus. All of a sudden an idea formed in my mind. Colleen had been relatively healthy up until last November when she got a real bad bout of Chicken Pox. She had to stay home from my sister's funeral because she was so contagious and was covered from head to foot.

Ever since then she seemed to keep coming down with things. Was there a connection? I made another mental note to mention this to the doctor the next time I saw him. I had already decided not to call him and let this flu bug run its course. He would think I was getting paranoid and I would feel foolish when he told me it was just the flu again.

Fortunately I didn't have any appointments at work, so I was able to slip out of the office without too much trouble.

"Hi Marilyn, I got your call, where's Colleen?"

"She just went to the bathroom; she'll be out in a minute"

"She's been awful sick lately. Are any of the other students away as much as her?" I asked her as Colleen came back into the room.

"There's so much going around, it's just that time of year."

"Hi Mommy" she said to me looking very pale as she got on her coat.

"Colleen, I'm starting to think this is all a grand plan of yours and you're not really sick. You just want Mommy to come and get you so we can go home and spend some time together. I think your Dad must be in on it too, because he never seems to be around when the school calls."

A smile crossed her lips and I could tell she thought it was funny what I'd said. At least there was nothing wrong with our "sense of humor."

At home I helped her into her pajamas and get settled on the couch. I took her temperature and was surprised to see it was so high. I got some Tylenol and a big glass of water.

"Drink this, Honey, to swallow the pill." Not long after my husband came home and I went back to work forcing myself not to call the doctor.

The next morning I noticed a strange rash on her skin and her cheeks were so rosy they looked like she had been slapped. I had seen something on her skin a few days ago, but I guess I had dismissed it. I realized that I had promised myself not to call the doctor, but the cheeks and the rash were enough to make me swallow my pride and pick up the phone.

"We can squeeze you in this afternoon, Sharon" the nurse said to me. Someone had just cancelled and my timing was perfect. It was a long wait during the morning and by early afternoon my imagination was running away with me as to the possible causes of her latest illness.

"I know what this is," said Colleen's family doctor, still examining her arms and tracing his fingers over the long lacy mottled rash under her skin. "The flu-like symptoms you described; runny nose and red cheeks, a high fever and along with this rash everything fits together perfectly."

"What is it?" I asked relieved and encouraged by the confidence with which he spoke. Now we were getting somewhere and hopefully to the bottom of this mystery.

"It's called Slap Cheek Syndrome, or you could also call it Fifth's Disease"

"How did she get that?" I asked never having heard these names before.

"It's just a virus that she picked up. It's probably in the school. Some kids get it others don't. It will run its course and should start to clear up in four to six weeks."

"Is there anything that she can take? What about antibiotics?"

"No, antibiotics don't work on viruses, she'll be fine, don't worry" he told me packing up her file and getting ready to leave for another patient.

"Thanks, doctor," I said wondering how many more strange conditions Colleen would pick up in her life.

Just last summer we had been on a picnic when the next day she had developed a strange looking rash on her arms and legs. The doctor had said she had "prickly parsley"; it was a plant that she must have brushed up against on the island we were picnicking on. To this day Colleen still thinks she has an allergy to parsley, and won't eat anything that has parsley in it.

I forgot to ask him about any connection to the Chicken Pox and her frequent illnesses, and much later I wondered whether coming into contact with this strange plant was actually the beginning of her health problems.

"Oh, and she shouldn't be around pregnant women. Sometimes this virus can affect the fetus."

Great! I thought. One of Colleen's favorite teachers was pregnant. I would have to call the school as soon as I got home and let them know what the doctor said. Also, I had to try to find some way to stress to Colleen that she had to be careful and to keep her hugs to herself until she got all better just in case she was contagious and could infect someone else with this strange, annoying condition.

EASTER, 2003

"What's that rash all over her body?" Were the first words out of my sister's mouth when she entered the house weighed down with bags and Easter treats. She had barely set one foot in the door and noticed right away something was wrong.

"It's nothing serious. Just a virus called Slap Cheek. The doctor said it should go away in a few more weeks on its own," I said in reply feeling confident that things would unfold as promised by the doctor. I was too consumed with trying to figure out where to direct everyone that came in the door that I didn't carry on the conversation further.

"I don't know, it doesn't look right, but I'll take your word for it," my sister relented as she set the heavy parcels on the counter.

The weather was unseasonably warm for the beginning of April and I felt that somehow we were blessed. With over 20 people in the house it was a relief for the kids to be able to play outside during the day and not be underfoot in the house.

Everyone pitched in and it was a memorable time.

Months later my sister-in-law was showing me the pictures she took from Easter and I wondered how I could have been so foolish. Everyone in the family other than my sister had dismissed Colleen's rash so easily. I guess that I had to put faith in what the doctors said, and I never questioned their diagnoses.

May, 2003

The beginning of May started out with more illness and more trips to the doctor. She was sent home with more assurances that she had just picked up another virus. At one point I thought of investing in shares of Tylenol and other fever control medicines. I had spent a fortune it seems each week on just trying to control Colleen's temperature and keep her in school.

The strange thing was that she wasn't "acting" that sick. She appeared to be charged with energy these days and was running on adrenaline. To confess, part of me was a little troubled with her behavior and her constant illness.

I have noticed over the years that my other children would get hyper and over-energetic just before they got sick. I guess Colleen was following their patterns.

Mid-May

"Idol's on" I shouted out as I brought the last of the snacks into the living room. It was the final episode of "American Idol" and tonight we would find out who was going to win. We all had our favorite and it was going to be two hours until we found out who had picked the winner.

The show was nearing an end when I reached down to caress my daughter's neck. Touching was a big thing in my family. I always felt it important to touch and say you loved each other. We hug hello, we hug goodbye, we hug goodnight. It's no wonder that Colleen became renowned for all the hugs she gave the nurses and doctors.

"Mommy, can you massage my neck?" Asked Colleen, already holding up her long mane of chestnut hair. She had beautiful thick hair that had a real shine to it. She was so proud of her hair. Now that she was a little older and could look after it on her own, I let her grow it as long as she wanted. Her favorite style was two ponytails sticking out of the top of each side of her head while the rest of the hair fell free.

I have always felt that if kids were allowed to express themselves and be confident when they were little, they would feel less of a desire when they got older to take extreme measures. I still don't know if this is true or not because my oldest is only 15. Only time will tell.

"Are you sore?" I asked running my fingers over the back of her neck. At first I wasn't sure what I was feeling. Trying not to be too intrusive to my little six year old I went back to feel the back of her neck as I played with her hair all at the same time.

"Mommy, that feels good, can you massage my back too?" She said as she leaned back into my hand. I thought it was strange that a child so young would suddenly develop aches and pains.

"Of course" I said, and proceeded to examine her under the guise of a mere massage. I moved my hands slowly and carefully over the skin. With each pass of my finger on flesh I felt as if I was looking for something that was hiding and that was trying to be elusive for a little longer. My mind was drawing conclusions and jumping to tremendous conclusions all the while I tried to concentrate on the television show before me.

I felt a lump at the base of her neck. I wasn't sure what I was feeling and my brain assumed it was nothing to be concerned about. However, I kept going back to the spot and each time I felt a nauseous feeling in the pit of my stomach. My mind reeled for an explanation. How could a lump be on her neck?

"What is it Mommy?" Asked Colleen starting to twist so I could no longer feel the intrusion under her skin.

"Nothing baby, just a bump." I said, trying to keep my voice as calm as possible. "Does it hurt if I touch it?"

She stopped squirming long enough for me to have another touch.

"No, not really," she said as she leaned back into me so I could continue the massage. "I can't feel anything."

Was this good? Was this a bad thing? I didn't know. All I knew is that my heart had started racing and my mind kept jumping to endless possibilities. Do I take her to the hospital now? Do I wait until morning? Do I ignore it?

"How else do you feel? Is your throat sore? Do you have a headache? Do you have a fever?" I blurted out the questions faster than she could digest my requests.

"I'm fine," was all she said.

I was remembering a time when my eldest had a lump on her skull. She must have been around the same age or a little younger. I felt it and thought it must be a tumor or something. I rushed her to the hospital and waited almost three hours on the Monday of a long weekend in May (coincidentally) for a doctor to rule out my fears.

As it turned out it was just a normal cyst that comes up from time to time on the scalp. I was convincing myself that this was the same thing and that I would lose not only precious sleep as I had to work in the morning, but also that I would look foolish for falling victim to the same panic twice.

The show had ended and the Idol was crowned.

"Time for bed young lady, brush your teeth and I'll tuck you into bed."

"Can I have a glass of water?" She said as I kissed her good night.

I looked a little more closely at her face. It looked swollen and she still had the red cheeks and rash. Hadn't enough time gone by? The Slap Cheek virus should be gone? Was she running another fever too? She had felt warm when I kissed her and I thought I could see swollen lymph nodes on one side of her neck. I was going to call the doctor the next day because we were supposed to open our trailer on the weekend. It was the first weekend of the season.

"Are you looking forward to the long weekend?" I asked her as she finished her drink.

"Yes. I want to go swimming and fishing. Will Auntie Colleen be there?"

"Of course she'll be there. This is her first season since she bought the trailer. It'll be fun. Also, it's supposed to be nice weather too." I turned off her light and went back to the other kids. I couldn't shake the feeling that something was terribly wrong with Colleen. I forced myself not to panic as I said good night to the other kids.

"I'm worried, Danny" I told my husband. He was dozing on the couch. He had just started a new job and was working a lot of overtime.

"I am too. But the doctors don't think it's anything too serious." He said stifling a yawn. I kissed him good night as he rose from the coach. I couldn't sleep and was hoping that watching more mindless TV would help me get tired and fall asleep.

Feeling sleepy at last I headed for bed. Thinking about the next day wore me out. What was on my schedule and how could I fit in a doctor's appointment? The discovery of these lymph nodes and she still had the lacy rash and rosy cheeks was very unsettling. Also, I had been noticing she had been sweating a lot during the night the last few months, and always kicking off her covers.

Was it still Slap Cheek syndrome? Could it be lingering like a parasite clinging tenaciously to the last vestiges of life? It had been well over the six to eight weeks the doctor had said. Maybe it was causing the swelling lymph nodes?

As I fell asleep I remember feeling like the shadows were moving and there was a storm coming that would wipe out our family with one strong burst of wind.

Morning

"Can you put on the kettle while I wake the kids?" I turned over to my husband who was still deep in the throes of sleep and apparently had not heard the alarm.

"Huh? Oh yah, sure," he replied still very dozy. It usually was a waste of time to talk to him about anything until he had ingested his daily morning dose of caffeine.

Several times over the years I have been angry with him for forgetting something we've talked about or claiming to have never been told. Finally I got smart and tried an experiment. The result was that I don't discuss important details before his first cup of coffee in the morning.

"Thanks Dan, I'm going to see how Colleen looks this morning. Maybe a miracle happened overnight and the lymph nodes won't be swollen anymore?" I said thinking that this was a farfetched wish.

Wednesday, May 14, 2003

I went straight to Colleen. She was still sleeping and I was hoping to have a closer look at the lymph nodes on the one side of her neck. She was lying on her back and now I could see both sides of her neck.

I don't exactly know how to describe the horror I felt when I saw that the lymph nodes on both sides of her neck were now grossly swollen. I reached behind her neck to check if the one back there was still a concern. It was.

"What's wrong, Mommy?" She asked stretching her arms above her head and pointing her toes to the bottom of the bed.

"Well," I started, choosing my words carefully. "It's not normal that you are so swollen in your neck, how do you feel?"

"I feel fine" she smiled as she sat up in bed. "Why?"

"I think we may have to go to the doctor today" I said dreading her expected reluctance at the possibility of missing more school. "Perhaps if you feel fine you can ride in on the bus and I can pick you up?" I offered hoping this would satisfy her.

"All right," she agreed, "but we are having french class today and I don't want to miss it." She loved her french teacher and since her older sister and older brother were learning french she decided she needed to learn to if she wanted to understand them talking. She hated not being in the loop.

I got to work and immediately called the Family Doctor. The answering machine said they were closed today and would re-open in the morning tomorrow. At this point wild horses could not keep me away from dealing with this today so I made plans to go to the local hospital emergency room and wait it out no matter how long it took.

I picked her up at school after her french class and we went to Emergency. Fortunately for mid-morning on a school day the wait wasn't very long and we got right in to the doctor. Colleen had just come from school and all her friends and so was boisterous and happy and full of energy and just wanted to go back to class.

"So what brings you in to the hospital?" Inquired the doctor to Colleen in a light, non-threatening way.

"She's got these swollen lymph nodes on both sides of her neck and behind her head. I just noticed the one in the back last night, and the others came up overnight. Other than that she's perfectly fine." I interrupted before Colleen could answer.

"Has she been sick with the flu? Does she have a sore throat? runny nose?" Asked the doctor looking at Colleen.

At this point the doctor didn't show any cause for alarm and I was starting to feel like an overactive parent once again standing before a judge who would convict me of over-protectiveness, over-reactivity, and plain, senseless panic.

"Well, she was diagnosed with Slap Cheek syndrome and she's supposed to be over it by now. That's the reason for her rosy cheeks and the rash on her skin." I said as the doctor started to digest these details and turned to Colleen.

"How are you feeling?" Asked the doctor.

"I feel fine" was all she replied, obviously getting bored with all the questions.

The doctor seemed to consider the list of symptoms presented before her and Colleen's overall health at the moment. She was not at all lethargic but rather pumped with energy. You could see the rash, red cheeks, and swollen lymph nodes, but other than that she seemed perfectly fine.

"I know what this is," proclaimed the doctor, "I've seen this before" she attested, "it's non-symptomatic strep throat" she said without even looking in her mouth for signs of redness or swelling in the throat.

"How can this be?" I asked perfectly puzzled. "Don't you think she'd have a sore throat?"

"Not always and there's a lot of viruses going around. I'm convinced this is what it is," said the doctor more reassuringly so my confidence in her diagnosis could be solidified.

I think back on this now and wonder if the doctor really knows that if she had taken just a little more time, had actually physically examined her belly to see how swollen her organs were, took a blood test or something, how she could have prevented the illness from going from stage one to stage four in a matter of days.

She didn't ask, in my memory, how long Colleen had had the Slap Cheek. However, I don't blame her; she was doing the best she could. Colleen wasn't acting sick, so it had seemed like a perfectly normal diagnosis to me, and I didn't question anything despite the fact that I had a terrible sense that there was actually something more sinister going on.

"I'll take a throat swab to confirm my diagnosis. In the meantime I'll prescribe some antibiotics. Check with your family doctor on Tuesday after the long weekend if things don't seem to change and to get confirmation on the strep throat. Have a nice long weekend," she said turning to leave as she now had other patients waiting as they started to trickle in slowly as the clock approached noon.

Chapter Two

May 17, 2003 Victoria Day Weekend

"What's for lunch?" Asked my son Ryan. "I'm starving," he said as she threw a ball in the air to Colleen who was eagerly waiting his throw.

"Meat and buns," I said as I unloaded the last of the bags from the car. We had just been to town to stock up for the long weekend. Our trailer is parked at Canoe Lake, but the town of Westport is nearby.

As I started to prepare lunch, I glanced out of the windows of our small trailer. The trailer had belonged to my sister and her family. They had purchased it in Alberta many years before. A few years earlier they had decided that they wanted more luxury in their holidays as the kids grew, and they kindly gave us the trailer, named Kelly, for my family to enjoy.

It was so peaceful at the trailer. The lake itself seemed to have a life of its own. You can feel the presence of long-ago Native Peoples that had inhabited the land.

It was so beautiful that I made up a story to the children that should they soil the land or the lake they would be visited by unsettled Indian spirits that demanded respect from the current inhabitants of the land.

I used to feel, and feel strongly still, that the lake has healing powers that go far beyond the scope of modern medicine. It was a place where healing and miracles happen.

It is so interesting to me now to know how right I was then in my assessment of our quiet country retreat nestled among the tall pines. We have tried to spend as much time there every summer as possible and it seems Colleen has benefited from the retreat.

"Mom, can we play with these bikes?" Asked Colleen already pushing an old mountain bike to the top of the hill where our old trailer sat.

"Just be careful," I said as I set about cleaning the remains of our lunch scattered over the picnic table. "That hill is steep and I don't want you to hurt yourselves. Stay away from the edge".

I watched them play for awhile and then went into the trailer to put away the dishes. My husband was busily trying to put together some fishing rods so we could try to catch some fish for dinner.

"These rods are all tangled together, it's a good thing I know what I'm doing or we wouldn't be fishing for days!"

All of a sudden I heard a loud cry and ran out from the trailer to see who was hurt. Danny was already on his feet and halfway down the hill. At the bottom of the hill, sprawled under the weight of the ancient rusting mountain bike, was Colleen.

While my back was turned, the two of them decided to ride

down the hill on the bikes! She hardly knows how to ride and her bike didn't even have brakes! What were they thinking?

"Are you OK?" I yelled as I ran down the hill, my husband already helping her up. "Why did you try to ride down the hill?" I asked with my voice taking on a stern tone as I noticed she didn't appear cut or bruised, just a little shaken.

It's interesting how fast parents can turn concern over the welfare of their child to discipline once they know they are fine.

"We thought it would be fun," answered Ryan who was looking a bit sheepish because I could see it was his idea.

"I'm sorry, Mommy," Colleen started to cry now not because she was hurt but because she thought I was angry with her.

"It's OK, sweetie, don't cry, at least you're not hurt. I don't want to see you doing that again until you're a lot older and have a better bike. It's very dangerous. You almost went straight into that tree. You could have broken a bone or got really hurt. It's too nice out to have to go to the hospital." I said as I helped her up and brushed off her knees and dirty hands. "Now wheel this bike back to the shed and put your bathing suit on, we're going swimming then fishing."

Colleen and Ryan walked the bikes back to the shed and went in the trailer to change.

"I can't believe they did that" I said to my husband, shaken. "I am imagining all sorts of possible outcomes that could have happened. Broken necks, arms, legs and lots of blood. It's just lucky she fell before she went over that second hill into the ditch or hit the tree."

I will never forget that moment for the rest of my life. It plays over and over in my mind like a tape set on auto-play. Today I am convinced that angels were definitely looking out for Colleen and helped cushion her fall.

I feel strongly that we were given the chance to have one last time together as a "normal" family without the worry of illness and fear of loss that would stay with us for the next few years. On the other hand, if she had hurt herself and we had needed to go to the hospital, would they have found the cancer sooner?

The rest of the weekend went smoothly. My sister arrived and took up residence in her trailer next to ours and we all had a terrific time together.

On the way home on Monday night I could still see the swollen Lymph nodes on Colleen's neck and her rash didn't seem to be clearing up despite all the sun on the weekend. I was feeling very uneasy as we unpacked the car and settled back home.

I had a sense of impending doom and I knew that there was nothing I could do to slow down the approaching disaster. It was a long time before I fell into a troubled sleep.

Tuesday, May 20, 2003

I phoned the doctor's office first thing in the morning, "The Emergency Room Doctor prescribed antibiotics that she has been taking all weekend, and she told me to follow up with Dr. Asemi on the results of the throat swab she took", I explained into the receiver hoping that I could bring in Colleen as soon as possible. There was a hint of panic in my voice that was hard for me to disguise.

"I have an opening around 11:00 is that good?" Said Allison the doctor's nurse. I could sense that Allison was also getting worried over Colleen's health because she had been back and forth so often in the last few months. "Don't worry, Sharon; I'm sure she's fine."

I picked a reluctant Colleen up at the office in her school and headed for the doctor's office.

"This does not look right" were the doctor's first words as he examined her neck. "Lie down on your back, Colleen, I want to feel your tummy."

As Colleen climbed onto the examining table my head started to spin. I didn't like the concerned look on his face so soon after the diagnosis made by the Emergency Room Doctor who didn't seem at all worried.

This was the first exposure I had had to the "wait and see" approach that is practiced so often these days in the medical field and, in particular, with Colleen's health.

The Emergency Room Doctor did not want to panic and so she took a perfectly normal approach to her condition by "ruling out" any serious conditions in favour of "waiting and seeing" if the antibiotics would do the trick. She did ask me to follow up with the family doctor, and now it was obvious why she wanted me to do that.

He pressed all over her tummy and did this tapping thing with his fingers on her stomach. Later I learned he was feeling if her liver or spleen were enlarged and this was the technique that could be used without ultrasound or scans. With each tap I could see the lines of his lips tighten and the furrow in his brow deepen.

"What is it?" I asked with a concerned look on my face.

"Colleen, you can sit up now", he said as if ignoring my question.

"I don't think this is strep throat. I have a friend in Ottawa who is a pediatrician. I want to make a phone call to see if she can make an opening in her schedule to see Colleen right away. Wait here while I make the call", and with that he turned and left the room.

Colleen was still sitting on the table and was lazily swinging her legs back and forth and banging the drawers underneath. She appeared to be restless and was trying to find ways to amuse herself while waiting to go back to school.

"Colleen, stop banging the table, it's annoying," was all I could say to her. I didn't know what else to say that sounded normal and not too panicked.

"Mommy, can we go now?" She said.

"We have to wait for the doctor to come back. He wants you to see another doctor in Ottawa because he thinks you may not have strep throat and he's not as qualified as this other doctor who only deals with kids and sees a lot more different things that could be wrong."

"I feel fine," was all she replied. "Why do I have to see another doctor?"

Saved from answering this question her doctor came back in the room. He seemed rushed. Likely because we had taken up more time than was allotted to us by then and he had a waiting room full of other patients patiently gazing at magazines tapping their feet trying to hide their displeasure at the longer wait they would have to endure before being seen.

It's not the doctor's fault; there are too many sick people, too few doctors, and so little time to help everyone. My doctor always did his best.

"The pediatrician said she will try to fit her in before she opens tomorrow. She can see her at 9:00 a.m. tomorrow. I really urge you to make this appointment if you can," he seemed to plead.

The first thing I thought of was how was I going to get more time off work for this? My husband had just started his new job and it wouldn't look good to his employer to take time off. I quickly pushed any obstacles aside. Wild horses couldn't have kept me from taking her to this appointment.

"I'll figure something out, we'll take it." I said with such conviction that the doctor seemed relieved at my words. After getting directions we left the office and I dropped her back at school and I went to work.

In the evening at home I relayed the information to my husband. I was trying not to seem worried, but we both were feeling anxious. Instead of having an evening of worry, we opted to order a pizza, rent a movie, and watch it with the kids. We let them stay up late and prayed the movie would take our minds off the doctor's meeting the next morning.

Wednesday, May 21, 2003

After finally finding the office we arrived in time for our last minute appointment. The office wasn't open yet so there were no other people in the waiting room. We were greeted by the friendly receptionist who gathered all our pertinent information.

I could tell from her forced smile that she knew something I didn't about Colleen's health. I didn't suppose it was common place to take patients before the office opened and when it happened must be reserved for very serious cases. How serious a case was Colleen?

"Just take a seat and the doctor will be with you in a moment," she said as Colleen was already rummaging through the ample toy box in the corner of the waiting room.

As I watched Colleen play I was trying to reflect on the journey that brought me to this point. It was like I was in a long tunnel and walking slowly and in a straight line. Each time I came to the end of the tunnel it stretched out again in the distance.

I felt like I was living in a dream. Sounds and voices all seemed muffled and there was a surreal quality to all the people I met. The best way to describe it is like you are moving in slow motion. I think this is probably some coping mechanism for denial.

On some level I knew what was going on but, on another level, I was holding on to the fact there was nothing wrong. My conscious and subconscious mind was battling it out and resolved their differences in my dreams.

"She can come in now" said a nurse who appeared to be working with the doctor.

"Come on baby, you can come back to that toy in a minute," I said feeling a little guilty interrupting her play, it looked like she was right into her game.

"Coming," was her reply as she jumped up and held my hand.

I gave a history or her symptoms since March to the nurse. I started with the Slap Cheek to the non-symptomatic strep, to the night sweats, swollen lymph nodes, and now apparent weight loss. Just as I finished the doctor came into the room. You could tell she was a very warm person as she had a gentle yet reassuring nature that came out in her smile.

"How are you feeling today, Colleen?" She asked directing her question at my daughter.

"Fine" was all she said with a smile on her face. How many times would she say fine? Surely to goodness she must feel something or else we wouldn't be here with this specialist last minute on an unscheduled appointment.

This was the real beginning of my frustration over my daughter's apparent lack of discomfort with unpleasant things done to and inside her body. Most kids would complain of pain or something, but she never did. She just took everything thrown at her with a smile on her face.

I was feeling again that perhaps not only I but my family doctor was now overreacting to her symptoms. Hopefully this pediatrician could help us figure out what was causing these symptoms and we could get a prescription and go home to our normal lives.

The pediatrician asked all of the same questions over again that the nurse had. All the while she was looking at Colleen and I could tell she seemed perplexed. She asked her to lie down on the examining table and she proceeded to do the same "tap tap tap" trick on her belly looking for swollen organs with her touch.

"So, what did you do on the long weekend, Colleen?" She asked as she proceeded in her exam and wanted to distract her from any discomfort she may be giving her.

"We went to our trailer," she said.

"Really, did you have fun?"

"Yes"

Tap tap tap.

"Does this hurt?" She asked pressing down on her tummy to the side.

"No."

Tap tap tap.

"Does this hurt?" She asked pressing in another spot.

"No."

"And how does this feel if I press here?" She asked really pressing down harder in another spot.

"Fine," was all she said. That darn word again was starting to annoy me. How could she be fine when I could tell that the doctor was now looking worried?

"What did you do at the trailer?" She asked helping Colleen sit up.

"We rode bikes, swam, fished, and had a picnic."

"Sounds like fun."

"Then we came home and we played on our trampoline," she said as the doctor was now examining her neck.

A few moments went by without conversation. Suddenly the doctor said to Colleen "I don't want you riding any bikes or jumping on any trampolines for a little while until we can figure out what's wrong. Would that be OK?" Did the doctor expect a positive response from an active six year old that had the whole summer ahead of her?

"For how long?" She questioned, "Can I still play in the park and on the swings?" Colleen always had this way of trying to figure out exactly what she could do if something was ever taken away that she couldn't do.

This quality and curiosity really helped me and her during the course of her treatments.

There was going to be so much that she would not be able to do, and very little she could. We learned to make a big deal of the little things she was still allowed to do, and modify a few of the things she wasn't supposed to.

I'll never forget taking her to a matinee movie after leaving the hospital one day. She wasn't supposed to be around people because she was "neutropenic." This means that she was very susceptible to infection and couldn't be around people who might have germs and make her sick.

She really wanted to see this movie and I hated to disappoint her. She agreed to put on a mask, not touch anything, and go straight to her seat in the theatre, if she could go.

I checked out the theatre first and there was actually no one in that movie and very few people in the building at all. It was a school day mid-day and very few people were interested in seeing "Shark Tales" in the middle of the day.

We had a memorable afternoon, and her spirits were lifted, and we felt like conspirators because we did something that the staff at the hospital might have frowned on. (Actually, I bet they would have been happy, they just couldn't admit it out loud.) It turned out all right. Half the battle with cancer is someone's attitude and the same holds very true, especially for children.

"Well, perhaps if you play quietly and don't jump off the swings and play structure you can at least go to the park," was her reply as she already was beginning to realize she had better offer some alternative to this strong-willed child.

"OK."

"Sharon, I want to talk to you for a minute. Would it be fine if my nurse took Colleen back to the toys in the waiting room for a few moments?" She asked in the tone of voice that sounded like there was something serious she wanted to say.

"Sure. Colleen go with the nurse and play quietly. I'll be there in a minute," I said as she was out of the room in a flash and quickly resumed the game I had interrupted when we first came in.

"I have to admit I am not too sure of what this is. It's not Slap

Cheek because she's had it too long. She has physical symptoms but does not seem to be at all bothered. Her energy level is good and she doesn't act sick. I want to make a few phone calls to some colleagues. Can you wait awhile until I do a little more research?"

"OK," I said, suddenly realizing that even this pediatrician didn't know what Colleen had. I put on a smile and went to join Colleen in the waiting room.

After what seemed like an eternity the doctor came out into the waiting room. Several times earlier while on the phone to her colleagues she had peeked her head into the waiting room to see what Colleen was doing. All she was doing was playing with the toys.

"Well, I have a connection over at the Infectious Disease Department at CHEO. They have agreed to squeeze you in at 2:00 p.m. tomorrow. They will be able to identify if this is viral or bacterial as they handle a lot of cases on a daily basis. Can you make it?" She asked me, taking a seat. "It's hard for me to tell what Colleen has. Her symptoms all add up to something but her energy level doesn't fit"

Another squeezed-in appointment at the last minute? What was going on? Now I really started to get suspicious of what might be causing these symptoms. This whole process was really beginning to drag and wear me out.

It was now Wednesday and I had to wait until tomorrow to get more answers? The waiting was the worst part. What could we fill our time with tonight to take our thoughts off of the meeting tomorrow?

"Of course I can. What do you think it is?" I was mentally tallying up all the time I have missed recently from work. At least I still had enough vacation and personal days to cover another visit to the doctor. I sure hope my boss would understand that I had to be with her and couldn't leave this up to her father.

"I don't want to say too much, Sharon, and worry you for no

reason. Just go tomorrow and I'm sure you'll get some answers"

I dropped Colleen back at school and watched as she happily skipped back to the classroom. I stopped at the Office to inform the principal that she did not have Slapped Cheek Virus and that the teacher who is expecting need not worry about any contamination to the fetus. I then headed back to work and hit the internet.

It took me about 10 minutes to self-diagnose Colleen using Google. The ladies in the office told me that this was not healthy and that I was not a doctor. They said I was just worrying for no reason, and that probably what was wrong was very easy to fix.

One lady said Colleen's symptoms sounded like "Cat Scratch Fever" and that she knew someone who had it. I looked this up too on the internet, and while the symptoms looked similar, I couldn't help but feel this big foreboding and certainty that she had contracted Non-Hodgkin's Lymphoma because she had all the symptoms!!

"She has cancer, Debbie," I said to a co-worker who was visibly concerned for Colleen and was trying to calm me down.

"Don't say that Sharon, she's a child. Kids don't normally get cancer. I'm sure she'll be fine."

Thursday, May 22, 2003

We arrived on time at CHEO and managed to find the Infectious Disease Clinic. It was deserted just like the pediatricians office. Obviously these last minute appointments happened when the offices were closed or the doctors had a lunch break.

Looking back, I am very grateful that the doctors made personal sacrifices of their own time to help a child in need. Like all the doctors and nurses and staff at CHEO, they are so committed to helping their patients and families and often go above and beyond to do what is right.

The lady at the desk checked us in and we had a seat in the waiting room. She had that same knowing look on her face like the receptionist yesterday. Colleen went straight back to another set of Doctor's Office toys in a box and began playing. Not too long later a doctor came out and introduced herself. She escorted us into one of the private examining rooms, took out a big pad of paper, and began asking questions.

"Tell me some family history, Sharon. What illnesses are in your family and your husband's?" She asked as she readied her pen to write.

"Well, cancer is a big one in my family. My Grandmother had it. My mom died of it. My father died of it, my sister died of it six months ago. My husband's father died of it."

I felt like a robot answering these questions with little or no emotion expressed for the loss of my family. All she wanted was information and I was starting to see the connections forming in her mind as she scribbled lines on the paper.

"I see," she said drawing what looked like a family tree on her paper. "Any other illnesses?"

"Our hearts sometimes cause problems. My dad had angina and a quadruple bypass. My mother-in-law has angina too."

"So, tell me what symptoms you noticed first with Colleen, when did this all start?" She asked, politely smiling at me, and watching Colleen fidget out of the corner of her eye.

Here we go again, I thought. How many times and to how many people do I have to tell the same story over again to? So I started way back in November of the previous year with Chicken Pox that led into Slap Cheek syndrome (wrong diagnosis) to Non-symptomatic

Strep (wrong diagnosis) and so on.

"Has Colleen had a chest x-ray?" She broke in about a half hour later into the appointment. "I would like her to have one. Are you OK with this?" She asked looking at me with expectation.

"Fine," I said as I glanced at my watch. It was 3:05 p.m.

My other kids would be getting off the bus in an hour and a half and my husband was going to be working late. Hopefully this chest x-ray would go quickly and I could make the 50-minute drive home to meet the other children and get supper going.

I again was not thinking about what the doctor was wanting as my conscious mind kept denying what I was hearing and looking for ways to restore some normal routine. I should have asked why she wanted a chest x-ray in retrospect. Hindsight is 20/20 vision.

The wait was long for the chest x-ray because we didn't have an appointment. I realized we were squeezed in again because this was important to the doctor in Infectious Disease.

Finally they called our name and Colleen stripped down and stood naked from the waist up to be x-rayed by a large cumbersome machine in a dark cold room. This was the first of many more chest x-rays to come.

It still amazes me that the technician and I had to cover up with asbestos and stand behind a glass while my little six year old was standing there unprotected, absorbing the full effects of the radioactive beams over and over again.

I vaguely remember signing some sort of release form for the hospital allowing this procedure to take place and in fine print a list of the possible side effects of the test. Would a parent say no to a test that a doctor really needs to diagnose an illness and make your child better?

"We're all done. I'll send these reports right away to the doctor. Get dressed and go on back to the clinic," said the technician. I couldn't tell whether or not he knew something or not by the look on his face but he was doing his best to avoid my eyes.

It was 4:15 p.m.

Ella and Ryan would be off the bus. On the way back to the clinic I took a minute to call and tell them we'd be home soon. My oldest being 12, it was fine for her to look after my eight-year-old son for a little while.

It still bothered me though that I was so far away from them if anything should go wrong. I knew I was worrying unnecessarily but, considering what was happening, I guess I had a right to worry.

"Hi Ella, this is Mom. How was your day, Sweetie?" I asked in a light-hearted voice trying to disguise the worry that was lingering in my tone of voice.

"Good," was all she said. I have learned not to ask too many closed-ended questions if you want information from a pre-teen. She is a real good kid and not too much trouble but sometimes needs to be prodded for information.

"What was the best part of your day?" I asked probing a little deeper.

"Recess."

"What was so good about recess?" I asked starting to feel the pressure of time to get back to the clinic to get the results of the test. I didn't have the patience to play any games.

"Well, I got to play with my friends and we had a lot of fun."

She blurted out. All of a sudden she changed the subject

"Mom, can I have a new dress for my confirmation in June? My friends are all getting new dresses and their hair done." She started to ramble on in an attempt to ask as many questions without actually taking a breath between words. Now she was really talking because she was talking about wanting something. I have learned this is a common thread among teens.

"Ella, I'm at the hospital with your sister and I don't want to talk about this now. We'll talk later, OK? In the meantime please make sure your brother starts his homework and I should be home soon." I said, now really starting to get impatient to get back to the results of the chest x-ray.

This strange panic was starting to well up in my heart and I had no idea what was causing it to escalate. Now I know it was probably my sub-conscious kicking into high gear and sending out alarm signals.

I hung up the phone after saying "Hi" to my son and headed back to the clinic to await the results.

4:45 p.m., Thursday, May 22nd, 2003

We did not wait too long before the doctor that ordered the chest x-ray and another doctor I had never met came over to us in the waiting room. They both had this odd look on their faces. I could tell they were concerned about something and were trying to keep calm. I didn't need to ask them anything as they came right out and to the point.

"We don't know exactly what is causing the swelling of the lymph nodes. The chest x-ray shows a lot of swollen lymph nodes around the heart and in her chest." I looked at Colleen; she looked fine, no different than a minute ago before I knew her chest was full of swollen nodes. The doctor took me aside.

"We'd like to admit her right away and do some more tests. We are going to admit her to the oncology floor and start treating her as if she has cancer even though it's not been diagnosed." The doctor said this to me as I tried to register the words in order. Oncology? Cancer? Admit right away? Had I been right when I had looked up her condition on the internet yesterday?

"I'm sorry," said the doctor. "I know this is coming as a surprise to you and you were not expecting to have to stay at the hospital, but it's best for Colleen that we get to the bottom of this right away so we can start treating her to make her better."

The way the doctor said this made me wonder if I actually had a choice in the matter. Not that I would have disagreed, I often think what would have happened if I had not cooperated and insisted on going home with her. This was an "on the spot" admission. It must be very serious.

"How can this be happening?" I said to myself under my breath. All of a sudden I remembered my friend from town whose daughter had been diagnosed with Leukemia a couple of months ago. Colleen and she went to the same school. Was there an epidemic of cancer going on with children that no one has pieced together yet? I was numb from shock.

6:30 p.m., Thursday, May 22nd, 2003

"What are you putting that on for?" I asked the nurse who was putting a clip over Colleen's finger attached to a wire hooked into a heart monitor.

"The doctor wanted it put on, at least overnight" said the nurse as she continued hooking Colleen up to the machine. She taped the clip onto her finger so it wouldn't fall off. It shone red at the top to show it was working.

"Mommy, I don't want this on. Why do I have to have it? I can't move around if I'm stuck to this machine," said Colleen visibly upset at being trapped in one spot.

I looked at the nurse who was merely following doctor's orders and said, "We'll call it Rudolph. We'll pretend that the red glow is his nose. I'm sure we'll be able to take it off in the morning." I said.

Little did I know then how important that heart monitor was. Her heart was surrounded by lymph nodes applying such pressure that she could have gone into cardiac arrest or stopped breathing all together.

"I need to take some blood work" said the nurse pulling a large cart up to the bed where Colleen was now currently confined.. "I'll also need to put in an IV."

"Why does she need an IV?" " I asked.

"The doctor wants her to start getting some basic fluids intravenously" she said without explaining any more than that. She was trying to force a genuine smile but I could tell she knew something I didn't about how sick Colleen really was.

I have noticed that the sicker the children are the more pleasant are the doctors and nurses as they describe what needs to be done and what tests will be ordered.

I watched as she tried to find a vein to insert the IV needle into. The nurses had this down to a fine art. What must go through their minds day in and day out as they have to prick and poke such little children, even babies, and draw their blood and insert IV's.

"It's OK, baby, be brave. Mommy's here. Take a deep breath." I said trying to reassure my daughter. I think this was the first time in her life she had given blood. It was the first of countless hundreds of more times this would and will happen in her lifetime.

"I'm fine" she said, putting on a brave face and trying not to grimace. The needle didn't seem to bother her as much as being hooked up to the heart monitor and trapped in one spot.

Everything was happening so quickly. It was like being moved on a conveyor belt through different stations. Different doctors were coming from all over the hospital and out of the woodwork to check on Colleen, all the while asking the same old questions over and over again.

"We heard about these magnificent lymph nodes in your neck, and we've just come to have a look" said one doctor as he examined the ones in her neck with his hands. "Impressive" was all he said then turned to leave waving as he left the room.

I was starting to get the feeling that Colleen was turning into one of those "unique cases" that don't turn up very often, and the entire hospital was curious about her.

7:45 p.m., Thursday, May 22nd, 2003

I had managed to make another quick call home a couple of hours ago to let the kids know we were being admitted to the hospital shortly after I had spoken with the doctors. I was trying to keep my voice cool to avoid getting into any lengthy conversations with them.

"Hi, Ella, how are you? It's Mom. Did you tell Daddy we were at the hospital?" I asked as calmly as possible.

"Yes. Mom, why are you there?" She asked with just a hint of worry in her voice. "Is Colleen all right?" She asked and I could tell she was confused.

"She's fine, honey. They are just running some tests and they want her here so we don't have to go back and forth. They want to get to the bottom of the rash all over her and the swollen lymph nodes".

"Cool. Will you be home tomorrow?" She asked in such a way that I knew she wanted to ask another question.

"Hope to be. I know what you want to know. It's about the dress for confirmation, right? I promise that when I get a minute we'll go shopping in Ottawa, OK?" I said really hoping that I could keep my promise. I never make promises I can't keep, so I don't make absolute promises very often. The kids know if I promise something it's as good as done.

"Great. Hold on, here's Dad. Bye Mom, good night," she said obviously pleased with the new dress idea and no longer focused or worried about her Sister.

"What's going on?" Demanded Danny in a very concerned tone of voice.

I didn't know what to say. My mind went blank. I could feel the tears welling up in my eyes.

"Sharon, talk to me! What's going on?" He pressed even harder.

Again, I couldn't find the words. All of the pent up emotions from the day and having to remain calm and cool just came flooding up from the pit of my stomach. My head started to pound, my stomach felt sick, and I was having difficulty catching my breath. I felt like I was being sucked into some type of vacuum and the world was spinning out of control all around me.

"I'm coming to the hospital" he said ready to hang up the phone.

"No!" I finally managed "Don't come. You have to go to work

tomorrow. You just started that job and you love it. Also, one of us needs to be there to look after Ella and Ryan."

"What's wrong with Colleen?" He asked again and this time I detected a note of fear in his voice.

Finally shocked out of the spiral into hysteria I told him the story and all the events as they unfolded today. There was nothing but silence on the other end of the line and I couldn't tell if he was even breathing while I was talking.

"Is it cancer?" He croaked when I finished talking.

"They don't know yet. They are treating her as if she has it, but they have to do a lot more tests."

"When will they know?" He asked impatiently.

"If they suspect cancer then I suppose they will do the tests pretty quick. I bet we'll find out tomorrow." I said with a surprisingly composed attitude. "I'm going to have to call in to work sick. I couldn't work anyway, my mind is not on it, and I couldn't concentrate. Good thing it's Friday tomorrow. I'm sure we'll be out by Sunday and this nightmare will be over."

"OK. But I'm coming tomorrow after work if you're still there." He said with determination. For the next half-hour we kept on talking trying to downplay our fears, telling ourselves this was all a mistake.

I said goodnight to the kids and then hung up the phone to go back to Colleen's room. I actually was feeling pretty good and light hearted. Talking with the kids and Danny was so normal. Coming up with other causes that were not so serious helped me take the focus away from cancer. I got back to the room just as two doctors were leaving. They stopped me in the door.

"Mrs. Ruth. I'm Dr. Klassen. I'm one of a team of Oncologists here at CHEO. Can I ask you a few questions?" He said looking at me intently as he ushered me out into the Hall.

He then went on to ask the same questions over again that I had already answered to about a dozen different doctors by now. When did the rash start? When did the lymph nodes swell? What is my family history?

This question and answer dance went on for at least 10 minutes. I could see Colleen in the room behind the doctor looking worried and not very happy with the heart monitor attached to her finger.

"We'll be doing an MRI and a CAT Scan tomorrow. We also want to do a Gallium Scan" he was reciting tests I had heard about but never dreamed would be giving to my six-year-old daughter. "Depending on those results we will likely want to do a biopsy of one of her lymph nodes. The Surgeon will decide where to take the node. He'll probably take one from her neck because they are so prominent. We will also want to do a lumbar puncture to check her bone marrow." He said very matter-of-factly. I'm sure he tries to keep things as Professional as possible with his tone. I wonder if he realizes the catastrophic impact his words have on a parent?

"All of this tomorrow?" I asked, simply stunned at the long list of tests that Colleen would need to endure.

"Well, we'll have to see if we can squeeze her in. If you're in-patient you sometimes get tests done quicker than when you are out-patient." He said as if I understood the difference between in and out patient.

"I don't understand, what do you mean by in-patient?" I asked seeking at least a little clarification.

"In-patient refers to being admitted to the hospital" he said looking at me suddenly realizing that I was one of the new parents to this process, and not a seasoned parent yet.

I would soon learn all sorts of acronyms that would make it a lot easier for the medical staff to communicate procedure to me. For example NPO posted on a sign on your room door means that the child is not allowed eating or drinking anything because they have an upcoming procedure or test.

Colleen would have to be NPO to do her lumbar puncture. Fortunately the doctors try to do this as early as possible, but I have seen some children go an entire day without food because emergencies come up. It's no one's fault, just too many sick children and a priority list.

I was mentally ticking off the list of tests when I started to realize we may be here longer than I expected. "Dr. Klassen, do you have any idea how long we will be here?" I asked hoping for a good answer and praying it wouldn't be longer than a few more days.

"I don't know. It all depends on how fast we can get the tests and the results." He said glancing at his watch obviously mentally considering the remaining rounds he needed to do before going home. "And the weekend is coming and things slow down a little. We'll get the essential tests done tomorrow, but the remainder may have to be done next week. In the meantime we are treating Colleen the best way we know how. We don't want to do anything else too quickly because it's crucial we get an exact diagnosis."

"Can't we go home over the weekend?" I asked already knowing the answer but not entirely anticipating the reply.

"That's not possible. It's not a good idea. We want her here to keep an eye on. Monitor her vitals and continue with the IV fluids. Her chest is being compressed by enlarged lymph nodes; she could go into cardiac arrest."

I can't believe I just asked such a foolish question? Of course we couldn't go home. They thought she had cancer! They thought she was very sick! They were trying to protect her, not hold us prisoners!

What kind of mother was I? Why couldn't I get it through my thick skull that something was actually wrong? When would I get over denial? Why was I having a hard time grasping the actual reality of the situation?

Most parents would want their child to stay in hospital until they were better, wouldn't they?

"You're right, I wasn't thinking. I guess we'll just have to bring the family here," I said trying to make my voice sound festive. "We can all gather in her room and watch a movie or play a game," I said trying to look for ways to keep the family together despite the circumstances.

"No one other than parents can be allowed on this floor or in the hospital. The WHO (World Health Organization) has put restrictions on hospitals with the SARS outbreak. They've got guards posted at the front of the hospital now and I hear more restrictions are coming." He said now turning to leave onto the next room. "Her brother and sister can't see her until the restrictions are lifted" and with that he left.

I could see that he was just as frustrated as I felt. I wonder how many other families were complaining too. The poor doctor had to suffer the brunt and deliver the bad news.

I stood there motionless for a moment trying to digest what I had just heard. SARS? We were in the thick of it. It was all over the news. People were dying in Toronto. What a bad time to get sick. Now Colleen wouldn't be able to see her brother and sister or any other visitors. What if she picked up SARS? If she had cancer she was on the high risk list?

I wanted this whole thing to go away and prayed that we wouldn't be too long here. I didn't know what to expect and this was making me nervous. How was I going to communicate all this? When all I wanted to do was sit in a corner and cry. How I missed my mother at that moment.

Thursday May 22nd, 9:00 p.m.

"Just one more temperature and blood pressure reading Colleen, then you can go to sleep," said the nurse as she put the thermometer under her arm.

"Mommy, I can't sleep with all this stuff attached to me. My arm hurts and I don't like my hand being attached to this board," she said miserably from the confinement of her bed.

"I know sweetie, it's not fair, but the doctors want to make sure nothing happens to you overnight. Now, I have to go make a few phone calls so I want you to say your prayers and I'll be back in a few minutes. Mommy gets to sleep on that chair over there; it pulls out into a bed. I found some extra sheets in the hall and a pillow. You're actually the lucky one who gets the bed with that entire comfy mattress!"

Actually I was relieved that there was something like this chair to sleep on. I was prepared to sit up all night in a straight backed chair like you see in the movies. Unfortunately there was only one chair per room and the rules of the hospital allowed for only one parent to stay in the room.

At the drive-through in our local McDonald's restaurant there was a box that you could throw your loose change into that would help fund Ronald McDonald House. I finally understand the importance of this place first hand. It was a place for the rest of the family to stay if they lived out of town and had a sick child in the hospital. What an important place!

As I left the room and entered the corridor I was at once surprised to see that the lighting had dimmed on the floor. There appeared to be a whole new set of nurses and doctors milling around the nurses station in the center of the floor. I approached the counter and asked where I might find a phone to make some calls.

"Just around the corner to your right" said a nurse I had not seen before. She was twenty-ish, with long brown hair, a nice welcoming smile, and was wearing a multicoloured nurse's scrub that clashed with her funky earrings.

"Thanks," I said, "what's all the fuss about? What's going on with everyone here?" I asked wondering if there was some kind of emergency despite the fact the mood seemed light.

"We are just changing shifts. The night crew is in. We have a meeting with the day crew and exchange notes about the patients and how they did today. My name's Brenna and I'll be checking in on Colleen overnight," she said casually tossing her ponytail over her shoulder. "I'll take good care of her, don't you worry."

As soon as she said that tears started to swell in my eyes and I got all choked up. Here was this young nurse exposed to all this sadness day in and day out. How did she do it? How does she keep that smile on her face? What strength it must take from within to appear calm.

"It's OK, it's hard, I know. Don't worry, so much to take in all at once, and so unexpected."

"I'm sorry, it's just so overwhelming and I still don't know anything, and I'm so scared." I said trying to take control of my emotions. "I have to call my sister and let her know what's happening. Can you please keep an eye on her until I get back?" I asked

"Of course" she said, and with that headed off with a chart in her hand towards Colleen's room.

I was amazed to see that even among all this chaos there seemed to be a routine on the oncology floor. Each room I passed I could catch glimpses of children and their parents settling in for the night. TV's were being turned off, lights were turned low, and the last of the evening medications were given.

As I went in search of the phone to make some calls I was also reminded that I was in a hospital and that there were very sick children on this floor. A shrill blood curdling scream filled the night followed by tears and uncontrollable sobbing. All at once two or three nurses headed for the door to an isolation room where children who were immuno-compromized and very sick had to stay.

I watched as they ran in but didn't stay to find out what had happened. It was too much for me to watch. I learned later that the little girl staying in the room was upset about having to have another needle for a blood test and was putting up a fuss with the nurse who was only trying to do her job. Mom was unable to soothe her and so she started screaming in terror and pain.

9:30 p.m., Thursday, May 22, 2003

I dialed the number to my sister's house in Montreal. I knew she would be waiting by the phone, it only rang once.

"Hello?" Asked a raspy exasperated voice that sounded expectant and scared all at the same time. "Is that you, Share?"

I was again overcome with emotion and had a hard time forming my words and tears started streaming down my face. I barely managed but was able to issue a muffled "It's me."

"What's going on?" She demanded

"Well, we came in to the Infectious Disease Department, and now we are on the Cancer Ward" I said not believing the words coming out of my mouth.

"What?" Was all my sister managed to say before I interrupted her.

"We're not sure what she has but they are treating her like its cancer. They took a chest x-ray and now they have her hooked up to heart monitor, she's got her hand taped to a board with an IV in her and God knows what they have pumping into her now. They're going to do more tests tomorrow so I don't know what to tell you," I said, recounting the events as best I could.

"This is terrible," she said, "What do you want me to do?" She asked obviously unsure as to what to say.

"You can't do anything, Col. You can't even visit. There's a SARS restriction. I have no idea when I will be home," now I was starting to panic.

"Slow down, tomorrow's Friday. Laura and I will head to the house and check on the kids and stay with them over the weekend," she offered tying to calm my rising panic attack.

"That would be terrific. They don't know anything about what's going on. You will distract them. Please promise me you will try to keep things as normal as possible for them. I don't want them to worry if there is nothing too serious to worry about."

It was my sister who ended up delivering the news a week later to the kids that Colleen had cancer. I just couldn't do it. The words didn't want to come out of my mouth. Danny was in the hospital on his shift with Colleen and so my sister had made a special trip to break the news.

Ella and Ryan were upset and I think very confused. Over the last couple of years we had buried their grandpa and their aunt who had died from cancer. It was going to be a challenge to get them to have hope and not think that their sister was going to die as well.

"No problem. Do you want me to tell anyone else?" She asked offering to be the information source for the rest of the family.

"Would you?" I asked relieved at not having to make any more calls. "I'm exhausted."

"You go to bed now, I'll talk to you tomorrow", she said and hung up.

As I made my way back to the room I felt oddly disconnected from my surroundings. It was like a dream, a very bad dream, one of which I hoped I would wake up. I felt like the more time I spent in this dream world the harder it would be to turn back.

My hand closed on the door handle to my daughter's hospital room and I pulled open the door. Just beyond an array of blinking and beeping hospital machines lay my little girl.

She appeared so helpless curled up in the sheets of her bed. Despite all the wires and tubes attached to her she seemed to be sleeping soundly.

I made my way over to the makeshift bed and practically collapsed onto the pillow. I thought for sure I would be able to sleep, but it eluded me. As I lay there in the dark my mind kept racing over the events of the day.

I was being pulled down into the floor. My eyes were open. I could see the hospital room all around me. I tried to scream but had no breath. I struggled to sit up and catch my breath but could not move.

I finally managed to move my shoulders and said a silent prayer to God that I could move again. I knew that if I fell into the hole under me that I would never be able to climb out and all would be lost. For just the tiniest second I thought about giving into the feeling and wondered what it would be like to just drift away.

Then I thought of Ryan and Ella. I gathered my strength and tried as hard as I could to pull myself out. I felt myself start to slip and struggled even harder to get up. Just as I was about to fall farther and farther into the abyss I was startled into consciousness.

"Mrs. Ruth, its Brenna. You were dreaming. Are you all right?" She asked obviously concerned for me by the look on her face. "Can I get you something?"

As my eyes adjusted to the night around me I could make out her shape looming over Colleen in the bed. She was taking her temperature while she slept. I couldn't understand why her temperature was important to constantly monitor. It seemed there was always a thermometer in her mouth.

How naive was I at this time looking back. The thermometer was to become the gauge by which we lived our lives while she was on chemo. If the thermometer rose to 38 we were on alert. If, a half an hour later, it went to 38.5, we called the oncologist on call at CHEO. This usually meant dropping everything and all plans and heading into the hospital for a blood test.

"With counts like hers and that high fever she can die very quickly if you don't come in right away," stressed Dr. Klassen to me on the phone from CHEO. "You can't wait until morning, come now and I'll call the oncology floor and have them get an isolation room for you ready and send up some medicine."

We were over 50 minutes away and I prayed that his warning was just a warning and Colleen could hold out until we got to the hospital. It was a struggle to stay within the speed limit and to concentrate on the road to arrive alive.

I can't count the number of times we headed to the hospital at 2 a.m. in the morning. If the blood test showed her counts were low, we were admitted for up to five days until her fever came down. If her counts were good, we could go back home and hope that things would stabilize and would not have to go back again too soon.

I never forgot Dr. Klassen's warning and so for the rest of my life will forever be anxious when Colleen gets a fever. I know that there's nothing to worry about now, but I'll never get over the fear I had that night as I sped off into the night and left the rest of the family at home asleep. That time, we didn't come home for almost two weeks.

"Is everything all right? What's her temperature?" I asked getting concerned by the sweat beading on Colleen's upper lip.

"It's a little high, 39.2, I'm going to give her some Tylenol to bring it down."

"What's causing it?" I asked, she looked so peaceful sleeping and not at all sick. "She has been having these night sweats for awhile; they must be causing the temperature to go up?"

The nurse looked at me but did not answer. She didn't know what to say and wasn't allowed to say anything. I'm sure she's seen these symptoms several times in her time at the hospital, but was not allowed to make any medical diagnoses.

Her job was to make sure the patients were comfortable, and to administer the chemo and drugs as prescribed by the doctors, not discuss medical issues with parents. But I could tell by the look on her face that she wanted to comfort me with answers but knew it wasn't allowed. What a terrible struggle of emotions for this warm caring nurse to have to endure day in and day out.

"I'll be right back with that Tylenol," she whispered as she left the room.

Friday, May 23, 4:30 a.m.

"Ouch," I thought as I tried to move my leg. "That hurts." I looked down at my leg. In the night I had twisted it in the covers on the cot. My back was sore and my arm was numb where I had been laying on it.

Everything was still dark. I moved my eyes around the room. Everything was still the same. Colleen was fast asleep in the bed and I could hear the familiar drone of the IV drip. Blip, Blip, Blip, Blip, Beeeep. Blip, Blip, Blip, Blip, Beeeep. That was a sound that I have come to realize I will never forget. Oddly comforting during the wee hours of the morning, and equally haunting in dreams and memories.

I noticed movement in the corner of the room. It was the nurse again. She was taking blood pressure and temperature readings. I guess I had drifted off to sleep. I now felt guilty that I had fallen asleep and she was awake looking after my baby. I struggled to free my legs of the confines of the bed sheets.

"I was just getting up to check on her." I said, rising from the cot.

"She's fine, I have been keeping a close eye on her" said Brenna looking down at Colleen in the bed, "She certainly likes to kick off her covers."

All I could think of was how inadequate I felt in the face of this young nurse. This was my child, and I had fallen asleep. All of a sudden I became very grateful for her presence. She worked tirelessly to ensure her safety.

At that time I did not realize how stretched the nursing staff was on the oncology ward, and how the increasing number of new cancer patients was putting a strain on the staff on the floor. They did their best with all they had to give.

Looking back now, I realize how important it is to have a relative stay with the kids while they are in the hospital. The chemo the kids were getting was very toxic and could cause all sorts of complications. There just aren't enough nurses to keep an eye on the kids 24/7. Besides how could any parent leave their child? I knew I couldn't.

"Thanks," was all I said, then laid my head back down on the pillow and turned over on the cot and cried silently into the pillow.

6:30 a.m., Friday, May 23, 2003

"Mom, are you awake?" I heard a voice from the other side of the room "Are you there?" Asked Colleen from her bed.

"Good Morning, Honey, I'm wide awake. How are you? How did you sleep?" I asked as I cleared my throat as I had been quietly sobbing for the last half an hour since the day and night shift started to change over.

"I'm hungry."

"What would you like to eat?" I asked wondering if the kitchen would be open at this hour. "What if you wait till 7:00 and I go down to the Cafeteria?"

"OK"

I walked over to the bed and looked down. She seemed so frail today. Really she was no different than yesterday, except for the fact that I knew there was now something very seriously wrong with her.

I looked at the rash on her skin and wondered how I could have let that go on so long? It wasn't a normal rash. I then reminded myself that I had done everything I could of by continuing to go back to the doctor. I still couldn't shake the guilt no matter how hard I tried.

"Move over, young lady," I said as I tried to slip in with her on the outside of her bed. I managed to get halfway in and actually snuggle despite all the wires and hookups.

"What's on TV?" I moved the suspended TV monitor towards the bed and pushed the button to turn it on.

"I don't care." She said very quietly. I could see she was thinking about home and what her and her brother liked to watch in the mornings.

"You and Ryan watch Scooby-Doo, right?" I asked knowing what the answer was.

I turned the dial and found the program just starting. Colleen settled back into the pillows and I laid my head beside hers and held her hand. As she watched Shaggy and all the gang fight ghosts, I wondered about the things we would face today and what answers would come.

I closed my eyes for a moment and opened them quickly. Nope, not a dream, this was a nightmare and now the entire day beckoned before us with endless waiting and unanswered questions.

9:30 a.m., Friday, May 23, 2003

"My, you're brave, Colleen. I wish all my patients were as good as you when I have to take their blood," said the nurse as she carefully inserted the fresh vial of blood she extracted into a special container.

"It's like she doesn't feel too much pain," I stated, "she has a high pain tolerance I guess."

As the nurse left the room she reminded us that the doctors would be doing their rounds shortly and we will know more about the timing of her tests. I watched her add some notes to Colleen's chart and leave.

I mentally counted the number of times Colleen had given blood since being admitted last night to the hospital. I added up five times. I reflected on why, when she was going back and forth between doctors before coming to the hospital, there were never any blood tests ordered?

What was it that they saw in her blood that made them want to continue to do more tests? And how come there were never any blood tests ordered before? I must remember to ask.

I heard them coming from inside the room. Their footsteps were sure and direct. They stopped outside the door and I could hear some muffled discussion. Colleen and I exchanged glances and were a little apprehensive about what to expect next. The door opened:

"Good morning, and how are you today?" Said Dr. Klassen coming over to the side of the bed wearing his best mid-morning smile. "How did you sleep?" He asked looking directly at Colleen.

Was he avoiding my eyes? I couldn't tell. I now have learned that one of the tricks of finding out how the children are doing is by talking to them directly. Parents have a tendency of speaking for their children, but a child who is gravely ill needs to communicate directly their feelings. He wasn't ignoring me.

"Gooood" said Colleen quietly from beneath her covers.

"Good? Well that's great. You look great." He said as he turned to the other three doctors in the room. "She came in with massive lymph nodes around her neck and this lacy rash on her body," he said as he held up her arm to show the other doctors.

"How long has she been presenting with these symptoms?" Asked another doctor to me obviously amazed at Colleen's relative good health despite her physical appearance.

Here we go again, I thought, and the questions and answers floated off my tongue like rhetoric. Perhaps I should ask for a tape recorder and then the next time another doctor comes in to see my daughter I'll just hit "Play."

"They are waiting for you down in MRI. We've also got a CAT scan this afternoon scheduled. An orderly will be up in a minute to bring you down," said Dr. Klassen calmly to me.

"OK," was all I managed to say.

"Once we get the results we'll let you know." He said and turned to leave the room, but before he did he cast Colleen a warm re-assuring smile.

"Mommy, will it hurt?" She asked me looking a little scared.

"I don't think so, Honey; it's just a test where they take a picture of your body." I replied hoping that I was right in my assumptions.

10:30 a.m., Friday, May 23, 2003

The orderly who came to bring us was dressed in blue hospital scrubs. His name was Adam. He was in his early twenties with curly brown hair and Colleen took an instant liking to him. He was charming and funny and did a real good job of taking Colleen's mind off of the impending procedures.

As I watched him interact with my daughter and wheel her down the Halls with the IV pole in one hand and her wheelchair handle in the other I was again reminded of the tremendous strength it must take to work in a Children's Hospital.

Here was another example of the kind of special people I was starting to find all over the hospital and how they worked tirelessly to help the Children and make their stays that much brighter and less scary. This place was filled with silent Heroes.

"Do you need some help Adam?" I asked as we were nearing a corner. "I can push the chair," I offered.

"No thanks, I have this down to a fine art. It's easier to push the IV and chair at the same time by the same person." He said casting a quick glance at me over his shoulder. "Here we are anyhow," he said as we approached the MRI department.

"Colleen Ruth is here!" He proclaimed to the receptionist behind the desk "Her Highness has arrived." He said looking at her with a wink of the eye and a smile.

"Well, well, Royalty, huh? Let me see, oh yes, here she is. You can go right in now Colleen, they are waiting for you." Said the receptionist playing along with Adam. "Mom, can you sign this release form before going in first though?" She asked trying to take on a slightly more serious tone.

I looked at the paper and then at the receptionist.

"It's standard procedure. It states the possible risks associated with having the tests. It's more of a liability issue for the hospital about full disclosure," she told me starting to sound like she was searching for an explanation and uncertain about how much she should say.

I scanned the page quickly and read the possible side effects. What choice did I have anyway? Without the tests the doctors wouldn't know what was wrong with her. I wonder what happens if parents don't sign this form, yet the test is necessary to confirm diagnosis.

"Here you go," I said as I scribbled my signature on the bottom of the page thinking that surely nothing serious would happen as a result of these tests but silently crossing my fingers at the same time.

Colleen was again a model patient. She smiled and laughed and obeyed the nurses and doctors very well. She lay still when she had to, she held her breath long enough when she had to, she gave blood willingly when she had to, and she never objected to the constant poking and prodding done by so many different hands on different parts of her body.

We were back in the room about an hour later.

The nurse and orderly helped settle Colleen back into bed. She looked a little tired to me, and she was saying she was hungry. Thanks to the generosity of many people who support the Children's Hospital, our room was equipped with a TV, VCR and DVD player as well as various types of video games.

I went in search of a movie to put on and to find something for her for lunch.

"There is a menu by the phone in the hallway." Said the nurse. "You can call anytime until after dinner tonight and they will send up food for the kids. It's a new way of doing things they are trying out. Sometimes the kids are too sick, or are in a procedure, or are NPO and the food would go to waste if it automatically came"

"That's a good idea," I acknowledged not fully appreciating what she meant but confident I would soon find out whether I liked it or not. At least I could cut down on costs and only have to buy food for myself. Even that was cutting costs because since we were admitted I had no appetite at all.

Later, when Colleen had started her treatments, she had actually been photographed showcasing this new way of doing things. I still have the picture of her in her hospital bed, eating lunch, dressed up like a princess.

I made my way down the hall to the phone. It was about 12:00 noon. I felt like I was in a time warp. I looked out the windows to the parking lot below and could see people milling about their daily lives.

Time was very off for me. Sometimes it stood still as we waited for the next test, and at other times was moving too fast as more answers became known. I wondered what Danny and the kids were up to. I wondered what was going on at work.

French Fries, Poutine, Subs, Cookies, Chocolate Milk, Ice Cream, Soup, Carrots, Celery, Hot Dogs, Hamburgers, the list went on. This was the menu from which to select Colleen's meals. It was certainly a kid's menu. I guessed that nutrition wasn't a big concern.

I learned later that nutrition wasn't a high priority at this point for the kids, it was more important that they eat anything to get nourishment between their chemo treatments and sickness. Why not tempt them with the things they should like? It made perfect sense to me.

I ordered some poutine and soup for Colleen and headed back to the room.

"Wanna black eye?" She asked to Colleen with her back turned to me. "How about a brown eye?" She chuckled as her body bounced up and down.

"Mom, look, it's Molly Penny, she's a clown, and she wants me to go to the playroom" Colleen blurted obviously thrilled to have a clown in the hospital. "Can I go?" She implored.

What was a clown doing in the hospital? Now I was thinking about the Stephen King book I read called IT where this evil clown attacked the children in a small town. She didn't look threatening at all. I quickly dismissed this thought.

She was about the same height as me and was very jolly. She had huge clown shoes on five times bigger than her feet. Her costume was brightly coloured and she had makeup and a big smile all over her face. She carried with her what looked like a big tool box covered in stickers and pictures and held all sorts of treasures.

I had not expected this visitor but couldn't but help feel uplifted when I saw her. All at once any uneasiness I was feeling disappeared.

"Hi, Mom, my names Molly Penny. Did anyone tell you about

the play room here?" She asked knowing that we likely hadn't had the chance to explore yet.

"I can't remember to tell you the truth. I have met so many people and have been told so much it's hard to keep it all straight. We got here last night, and then this morning we were in tests. I just ordered lunch and we were going to put on a movie" I replied. "What's in the playroom?"

"Well, each floor has a playroom. There are Child Life Workers there who, with the help of volunteers, do arts and crafts with the kids when they are well enough to leave their rooms. One of the more popular things to do is cook. Do you like baking cookies, Colleen?" She asked looking at Colleen with her big clown smile.

"Yes, Mommy and I bake Christmas Cookies with Ella and Ryan every year." She said looking excited about the possibility of baking cookies in a hospital.

"That's great, because I hear they are baking some cookies later this afternoon." She told her. "Mom, what are her counts? Can she leave the room and go to the playroom?"

"Ah, well, I don't know. I'm new at all this." I said miserably realizing there was so much to become accustomed to.

"Don't worry, I'll check with the nurse, and if it's OK I'll be back for you Colleen. Mom can take a break while you're in the play room and go and get herself something to eat. How does that sound, Mom?" She asked.

I realized that she kept calling me "Mom" because she had so many names to remember and clearly didn't remember mine yet. It was amazing how she had mastered Colleen's so quickly!

I thought about taking a few moments for myself to think. I didn't have much of an appetite but I needed to try to sort some of this out in my head. I reluctantly accepted the offer - feeling guilty for leaving, yet trusting her enough to leave Colleen for a few minutes.

"Sounds great, Molly Penny."

Molly Penny is actually a nurse in the hospital. She works part-time in the Operating Room and part-time as a Therapeutic Clown. Her salary for clown work is funded by an anonymous donor who believes it's very important to have this resource for the kids and the parents. Thank you whoever you are, Molly Penny is a godsend.

The Waiting, over the weekend to Monday, May 26, 2003

Not much more happened over the weekend. There were endless phone calls to family and still no answers to give. Next weekend would be Ella's Confirmation and Ryan's Birthday. What would happen between now and then?

"Wake up Colleen. Can you hear me? Wake up!" Insisted the nurse as she gently shook Colleen's shoulder. "You can wake up now," she urged hoping to see some movement under the covers.

Colleen had just had a biopsy of one of her lymph nodes. The surgeon had been by and examined her for an appropriate node to biopsy. At first we thought he would go for one in her neck as those nodes were really enlarged. He decided to take the node from under her arm pit. It was very sensitive of him to consider scarring.

"She's got so many that can be biopsied; I think I'll take one from her armpit so that way you can't visibly see the scar."

"Thank you," was all I could say. I had the sinking feeling that when a surgeon has "selection" to do a biopsy that it was not a good sign. They had already done a lot of other tests, and this biopsy would lead to conclusive proof that she had cancer in her lymph nodes.

"Mommy?" I heard the whisper escape her lips, "I'm thirsty and my throat hurts." She murmured trying to shake off the fog of the anesthetic.

"They put a tube down your throat while you were asleep so you could breathe, it should be all better very soon. I'll get you some ice chips to suck on," I said moving to the bedside table where the nurse had already brought ice chips in anticipation of her thirst.

As I looked down on Colleen in the bed a terrible sadness overcame me and I had to fight hard to keep back tears. How could this be happening? Am I dreaming or did my child just come out of a biopsy operation? We had been through so much these last few days that one shock was blending with another and reality kept closing in with unrelenting force.

I can't remember to this day what test was done first but I do remember two tests that were done and I will never forget what Colleen had to endure for a mere child of six years of age. Like most children who get cancer, you can call them heroes. They are so brave and so cheerful while their little bodies are subjected to so much pain and discomfort. The first of these tests was a lumbar puncture, or commonly referred to as a spinal tap.

We were led into a small room off the hall on the oncology floor. There was a table in there and some surgical instruments. It didn't look like much of an operating room to me and I wondered how it would be possible to check her spinal fluid from such a small space. Perhaps I was thinking like I was in the movies and expected something a little more grandiose.

She had been NPO since last night. This means she was not allowed to eat or drink as she would be given a general anesthetic for this procedure. It was now 11 a.m. and she was getting hungry and anxious to get this over with. I was welcomed into the room and took a place at my daughter's side as she lay on the table.

"Colleen, I want you to take deep breaths. You are going to start to feel sleepy." Said the anesthetist into her ear as she adjusted the oxygen mask over her face.

"It's OK Sweetie, Mommy's here" I choked trying to look and sound brave as she drifted off into sleep. As soon as she was out and her vitals checked the oncologist took out a large needle. It must have been over a foot long!

She turned Colleen on her side and ran her fingers along her spine searching for just the right spot. She appeared very skilled and knew exactly what she was looking for.

"Right here" said Dr. Mandell and with a swift motion inserted the needle into her back. I had to turn away as I couldn't watch anymore. I felt gorge rising up in my throat and I struggled to get control of my nausea.

"All done, we'll have the results shortly Sharon, are you OK?" She asked. I could tell I wasn't the first parent that looked like they were going to faint at what they just saw.

"Yes, just a little dizzy. How can you do this? It must be very hard?" I asked her as I started to back out of the room.

"A lot of medical school," she said with a smile, "and a lot of practice"

This was one of many lumbar punctures Colleen would endure over the course of her treatment. They did this same procedure to inject chemo into the spine to try to stop the cancer from spreading to her brain. They call it "intrathecal," and the chemo we got was called "Methotrexate."

Thanks to years of research on other children with similar cancers it was found that routinely injecting chemo into the spinal fluid while simultaneously testing for leukemia cells was an effective way to prevent "relapse" in the central nervous system. At least that's what I'm led to believe from what I've read.

Unfortunately it's a painful experience and Colleen's back looked like a pin cushion for awhile until the needle marks faded. However, despite the pain the good news is that it worked. It was two years later when we found out that things can go wrong in these procedures. Suffice it to say we're glad she has no more scheduled.

"She has to drink this dye before her test tomorrow or it won't work," insisted the nurse who was starting to lose her calm composure. "The doctor has ordered the gallium scan for first thing, and it is very important she drink this down now!" She ordered.

At first I was taken aback. This nurse seemed to be coming unraveled. It appeared that she was worried that Colleen wouldn't take the dye and that somehow she might get in trouble with the doctors for failing to do her part.

"Colleen, come on sweetie, take a sip" I pleaded.

"Mom, it's making me sick. I don't want it," she said stubbornly closing her mouth. "It's making me gag."

Of all the things that she had done to her to this point, including the fact that her veins were now collapsing from the constant blood tests, she wouldn't swallow this liquid? Perhaps this was a small attempt at rebellion and one small win for her to keep her in control.

"Drink it." Said the nurse looking directly at her.

"I can't swallow it," she replied.

The nurse appeared to be contemplating something then left the room. A minute later she came back with something called an NG Tube and another nurse.

"Well, if you can't swallow it on your own, we still do need to get the liquid into your belly for the test tomorrow. This is a tube and I'm going to put it down your nose and down to your stomach. That way you won't have to swallow," she explained thinking her solution was a logical one.

Reluctantly Colleen agreed to give it a try. She really didn't want to drink the dye. Was she allergic to it?

"She's choking!" I cried, "It's not going down," I said to the nurse who was determined to insert the tube down her nose. "She's coughing and having trouble breathing!" Couldn't she see this too?

"She's fine. Let's try again" she stated starting to put the tube back in her nostril. "Come on Colleen, lots of little kids have this and they don't seem to complain, if you could swallow the dye we wouldn't have to do this," she explained to her.

I watched again in horror as the nurse tried to put the tube back in her nose. I could hear a loud drumming noise and I realized it was coming from within my head. My heart was pounding fast as I was trying to absorb what was going on around me.

I started thinking about something I learned in psychology in university about how far someone would go when instructed to push a button knowing that it sent a bolt of painful electricity to a recipient on the other side of a glass window. How long would someone unquestionably obey orders before their own common sense kicked in and they realized what was happening?

"You hold down her arms," the nurse said to her companion. "Mom, you try to hold her head steady while I try to get this tube down her," and with that the other nurse came over and held Colleen's hands steady at her side. I went to the top of the bed and tried to hold her head still.

Colleen started to thrash about on the bed. She kicked her legs and arched her belly. The more she moved the tighter the grip on her arms and legs and the more we strained to pin her down.

I was now strangely disconnected from my body and watching the scene unfold from the roof of the room looking down. What I saw were three women and a little child. The child was in pain and agony and the women did not stop their intrusions into her body with the rubber tubing. She was gagging and appeared to be unable to breathe.

Panic was evident on her little face as she struggled helplessly to get free.

"Stop it!" The words came barreling out of my mouth. "She can't breathe. Her nose is clogged. She can't breathe through her nose. This isn't going to work" I said finally taking control of the situation.

I felt ashamed of myself for allowing this torture to go on as long as it did. What kind of mother was I? What kind of nurses were these? I don't care if the doctor wants this test or not, there has to be another way. On top of everything we didn't need to psychologically damage my child.

As if slowly emerging from a dense fog the nurse's vision started to clear and she was able to assess the situation more clearly. Gone was her driven determination to fulfill the doctor's orders and get the dye into Colleen for the test, and returned was the compassionate helping caregiver that we had encountered earlier in the day.

"I see what you mean. Her nose is clogged and she's coughing up all sorts of mucus. This isn't going to work," she said putting away the NG tube and wiping Colleen's nose.

Relieved that no more attempts would be made to hold Colleen down and forcibly insert a tube into her belly I asked "now what?" In the hopes there would be another more peaceful alternative.

The nurse just looked at me and didn't know what to say. What could she say? She had her orders and knew that she would have to write down that she had failed. I could see that this was bothering her, but I also sensed that she knew it was wrong to force it any more.

I didn't blame her. I know she was trying to do her job and I know the amount of pressure she must be under. The horrible things these caregivers have to do to the children for their own good is beyond comprehension to anyone who has never walked the Oncology floor. I decided that I would make sure she didn't have to suffer defeat in the eyes of the doctors tomorrow.

"Colleen, try to drink this again, it's the only way to get the test done tomorrow." I pleaded hoping she still trusted me and wasn't angry at me for what happened. "Take a little sip" and with that she let me raise the glass to her lips. She too didn't want the nurse to be upset.

She took the tiniest of sips and swallowed the liquid. I could see it was horrible for her as she suppressed the urge to vomit all over the bed. "Good girl" I said stroking her forehead. "I'm so proud of you and I'm so sorry you had to go through all that."

I stayed up the rest of the night. Every 10 minutes I raised the glass to Colleen's lips until the last of the liquid was gone just before dawn. Every now and then the nurse would come back to the room to check on our progress and see how much of the dye was working its way into her system.

I struggled to keep Colleen awake long enough with each sip praying that she wouldn't get sick and all this effort would be wasted.

It turned out she had had just enough dye for the test to be effective. The nurse was happy as were the doctors with the results. Her body had lit up like a Christmas tree in the test. The dye outlined the cancer cells.

"I promise you, Colleen" said Dr. Chris to her, "You will never have to have one of those tests again. We have all the information we need"

Colleen never had to have anymore of those tests, but later we found out she had an allergy to the CT contrast dye. Maybe she knew that if she took too much of this particular dye for the gallium scan that she could have gotten really sick and that's why she defied the nurse so much?

This is the way I remembered it, I'm not entirely sure it's the way it worked out. There were a lot of things that happened and, for the most part, it all seemed like a nightmare so I guess it's normal to assume my memories take on the nightmare flare.

I think back to the wonderful nurse at the time, and how she was bright and cheerful and very capable. She was an older lady, with kids of her own that were grown.

I guess when you get to be a mom; part of you wonders whether your kids are actually telling you the truth about something they don't want to do, or whether they are pretending. There was a 50/50 chance Colleen was just being stubborn.

A lot of parents of critically-ill children get put in the same position I have noticed. We tend to overindulge the children because they are sick, and sometimes forget that they are just kids and like all other kids, are prone to the same games, tricks and manipulations as healthy children to get what they want. In this case, Colleen wasn't pretending.

The Routine of the next couple of days....

Waiting for all the testing to be done was hard. And even harder I discovered was the waiting for the results to be known. This is the time that you imagine the worst, and everyone tells you everything will be fine.

You have nothing to do but wait in fear. So much hope and support you get from friends and relatives and hospital staff that you feel a bit guilty for lending credence to your fears.

Yet with each passing hour you are constantly reminded of where you are and why you are there. Your child is sick, and they are treating her as if she has cancer, and you are not allowed to leave the hospital with her at all. No one is allowed to visit either. I felt like a willing prisoner waiting it out on death row.

As a defense mechanism and to pass the time I quickly established a daily routine. Children are good with routine, and so am I. It's a good thing to be good with routine if you have a sick child because if the child's chemo is not routinely given on schedule and on time, their chances of survival are much worse.

Colleen would wake up around 6:45-7:00 a.m.

At this time the day and night shift would probably be already changed over. The Day Nurse would be taking her temperature and taking the first blood of the day to go down to the lab to check her blood counts. She would give a urine sample and have her vitals monitored and measured. At this time of day we were allowed to take off her heart monitor, so "Rudolph" would be unattached from her finger.

I would ask her what she wanted for breakfast and would go and order it while I went down to the cafeteria to get myself a coffee. Usually I went down in my slippers and it was interesting to look at the other parents in their slippers too. It was a good way to see who had stayed the night in the hospital.

After breakfast around 9:00 a.m.

It was time to get dressed and make the bed. We had a comforter from home for her bed and many stuffed animals to keep her busy. Colleen would go to the bathroom in her room, and while in there, I would make her "hospital" bed as comfortable as possible and straighten the sheets and place the animals all around so she could easily play. When she was done in the bathroom, it was time to get washed.

"Come on young lady, let's go get out of this room and washed up. It's good exercise, too."

She would hold onto her IV pole we nicknamed "Blue" and together we would venture into the hallway in search of the shower bath. She was usually attached to an IV so it was awkward at times to get completely clean.

I could tell the nurses were grateful that I was bathing Colleen and taking over her hygiene care. They really didn't have enough time to do it, but knew it was so important for the kids to bathe and get out of bed. It helped their spirits and kept them fighting.

I remember overhearing a conversation between two nurses once. I guess you could say I was eavesdropping. They were so upset for this child because the parents were never around very much. I didn't quite hear why they weren't, but I'm sure there was a good reason.

The child didn't want to eat or get out of bed, only lie down and watch TV. They were doing their best to get volunteers and other staff to be with the child when they had to be with other patients.

About a year later I learned that the child had lost her battle with cancer.

The shower bath was well stocked. There was always fresh linen handy and Johnson's Baby Shampoo in bottles. I got a kick out of putting this baby shampoo back in Colleen's hair. When she was a baby I used it all the time because it did not cause tears. However, as she grew, we graduated to more sophisticated no-tear shampoo that was scented differently and came in uniquely-shaped bottles.

Every time I washed the shampoo from her hair I wondered if she would lose it and how I would be able to help her through. Very fresh were the memories of my mother in front of her bathroom mirror as I watched her pull clumps of hair from her head after chemo. I could see the picture of my sister with a kerchief over her head in my mind too. My Dad, well, he didn't have much hair to lose by the time cancer came into his life.

"Here's a towel to dry off. Let's get you dressed and head back to the room. The doctors will be making their rounds soon."

Before diagnosis there was very little the doctors could tell us and not much more they could do.

"We don't have all the results back, so it's better to be patient before prescribing something that won't work," said Dr. Klassen during our morning rounds

Usually this meant that I would not see the doctors again until the next morning and I had another 24 hours of which to get through living in uncertainty and constant fear for the worst.

The days stretched before me like never ending highways that go for miles and all you see in the distance is dark.

What made the wait even longer for Colleen and me was that one of the samples they had taken was inconclusive. This means that the sample was not adequate enough to arrive at a proper diagnosis. This was either a lab mistake, or just bad luck. In any case, there was not much more we could do but wait for the results after another sample was taken.

I remember clearly encountering a doctor in the hallway whom I had never seen before. He came up to me and said that he admired my determination and patience in waiting for the "new" results to be processed, and that I was doing the right thing by waiting.

I still have no clue what he meant. I didn't think I had a choice other than to wait. Do some parents get impatient and cause the medical staff grief as an outlet to let off their own steam? Human error does happen and it does no good to dwell on what should have happened and we have to deal with what we get.

When the results finally came I understood how important it was to wait. Dr. Klassen had said to me one day when he was leaving that he thought Colleen had leukemia, but that we needed to wait for the results to be sure.

I mentioned this to one of the nurses and she told me I must be relieved that she had leukemia. It was so much easier to treat than lymphoma and had a better prognosis.

It turned out Colleen had a rare type of very aggressive non-Hodgkin's lymphoma that normally affects African males and people over 60. I guess I shouldn't have been surprised considering all of the other strange illnesses she was supposed to have had. It was just another unexpected challenge to deal with.

The doctors were now able to start her treatments armed with the proper knowledge of what she had and how best to save her life with current methods.

Chapter Three

After rounds were made we were free to go. If your child's blood work that was taken first thing came back good, they had all the white blood cells and neutrophils they needed, you could venture off into the "playroom." By now, we were very familiar with the playroom and it was a highlight of the day and a much needed distraction for both child and parent.

The "playrooms" were equipped with all sorts of exciting things for the children. There were board games, video games, and arts and crafts. And, most importantly, there were always other kids. There were outlets everywhere so the patients could plug in their IV's so as not to run out of power and stop the flow of medications into their bodies.

In time, you came to know by the sight of the colour of the fluid going into the child whether it was chemo or something else they were getting. In truth, the word "Biohazard" on the bags was a dead giveaway, in addition there was the makeshift coverings on the bags put on by the nurses to keep the sun off the medicine from the windows because it could alter the properties of the chemo.

Colleen's favorite part was the cooking in the playroom and the visits from Molly Penny, the clown. She also loved the child-life workers who worked there as well. It was a magical place in the midst of so much misery and a motivator to get well.

Some days much later, we couldn't always go to the playroom. The Chemotherapy treatments would drop Colleen's counts so low that it would endanger her life to go out and about other children. The threat of infection was too great.

On the days we were confined it was hard. However between the child-life workers, the volunteers, her in-hospital teacher and Molly Penny it was bearable. Colleen didn't seem to mind all of the one-on-one attention.

I hated being confined. It was summer and there was sunshine outside and warm weather. I couldn't stand watching the sunsets from her isolation room. I tried to make the best of it and we would count the hot air balloons floating high over the city in the evenings.

Trying to cope and be supportive can be very exhausting and draining. I don't know when these positions were created, but I think that the social workers attached to the hospital are such a vital lifeline. I know some parents didn't feel comfortable with leaning on their social worker but, if it hadn't have been for mine, I'm not so sure I could have come through this as well as I did.

Her name is Denise, and every time I think of her I owe her an immense debt of gratitude. Her official title is a social worker and she specializes in pediatric oncology. She's employed by the hospital to give support and counseling to the children and the parents.

I know I could not have kept things together so well if it were not for Denise being there and helping me deal with the reality of our situation. She would help me communicate with the doctors and our nurse case manager, Deanna. They were not always available because there were just so many patients to see and treat. Denise would make sure that any concerns we may have had were brought to their attention. It was such a relief knowing that your voice was heard.

When I needed to really cry it out, I would go to Denise's private office just off the floor. This usually happened when something went wrong with Colleen and she was suffering some sort of complication from the treatments like a failing liver or blood in her urine. It became unbearable to put on a brave face and I needed to get away for a few moments to collect myself.

As soon as I entered the door the tears would start. She would get a warm blanket, and wrap it around my shoulders, and bring me cool ginger ale to sip. She used to say that the warm blanket and the ginger ale seemed to help other mom's, maybe it would help me. I have to admit it was comforting.

"It's OK Sharon, let it out. There's so much to deal with. Colleen needs you to be strong, and it's healthy for you to get these emotions out." She would say handing me tissues and adjusting the blanket.

Eventually it would stop. I would have no more tears today. We would chat for a moment and I would feel a lot better. I was feeling stronger, and ready to go back and face what needed to be faced. Denise still keeps in touch to this day and always has reassuring things to say that help me keep my emotional glue sticky.

The playroom would be closed for lunch around noon for about an hour.

We would head back to the room and I would order her lunch from the menu in the hall. We would have selected a movie from the playroom and I normally put it on while she ate. I would get a few moments when she was distracted to think about everyone else at home and how they were.

It was so hard being apart. Some people say cancer brings a family closer together. It seemed to me that all cancer had ever done to me and my family was tear us apart both emotionally and physically! I suppose the fact that Colleen couldn't have any visitors didn't help either.

Spending so much time in the hospital can play tricks on your mind. You have no real sense of time and all your time is spent waiting for the next test. You worry about the outside world on some level, and how everyone is coping, but you are consumed with the moments that pass and all the new information you need to process.

There is a hustle and bustle in the hospital that becomes your life and you have little time for the reality you once knew and the things you had planned before you came in. Every hour that passes is packed with so many conflicting emotions that by the end of the day you are drained and exhausted and pray for a moment's peace and for the nightmare to end.

You worry about any other children you might have at home, and pray that the people at home are taking good care of them. Strong family support is very important. Fortunately we had some good support initially or things would have been much harder on the other children. I had heard some real horror stories from other parents and at least we didn't have to endure their hardships.

After Lunch most days …

"How can a cancer diagnosis be a gift?" She asked, suspicious that I had almost entirely lost my mind, "And, if you're right on some philosophical level, I want someone to take my gift back to the store, I never asked for it, and I don't want it!" Replied Kelly who was sitting on a couch in the playroom.

I had met Kelly and her husband Brian in the playroom earlier that day for the first time. The playroom was now open again that lunch was over. Their daughter Ashley who was also six years old and lived in North Bay had been airlifted to the hospital and they were just starting her "standard" tests to diagnose her type of cancer.

Most kids are very resilient, even the ones who are gravely ill. Ashley had wanted to go to the playroom to meet other kids too, just like Colleen. In between her tests she wanted to spend as much time as she could out of the room and with other children.

"Well, I don't mean that cancer is a gift, what I mean is that a diagnosis of cancer seems to bring out the best in people." I tried to explain to her that I've seen what cancer does to families and sometimes it brings people together. "I just got a phone call from a friend I haven't talked to in awhile. She lives far away. Someone from my husband's family knew her and put in a call to her to tell her what was going on with Colleen. It was so touching her reaching out. She said she didn't know what to say, but just that she was thinking and praying for us"

"That's nice," Kelly said, "I guess I know what you mean. As soon as they said we had to come to Ottawa it seemed everyone in the family has called and my best friend says she has been getting calls from all our other friends for news. I can't talk to them now, it's too emotional and, until we find out what's going on with Ashley, Brian has been asking people to hold off. Everyone's being so supportive it's really nice."

"I guess the gift is love then. The illness is an opportunity for your friends and family to reach out and all become reconnected, catch up." I was thinking about the reality of my words and it made me sad. Why did a tragedy have to be the reason to keep in touch? I guess as we get older it's really weddings and funerals that keep the family connected.

"Sharon, I think you're stretching now. Are you sure you're not taking any happy pills?" She said to me with a chuckle. I guess I was a little too prophetic.

"Then there's the gift of generosity. I hear from Danny that people are dropping food off at the house and at the Bank where I work. He says there's so much he won't know if they can eat it fast enough. His sisters and mom are coming out this weekend to help out with Ella's confirmation and Ryan's birthday, so I guess he won't need to shop!" I said, trying to make light of the fact that I was starting to realize I may not be home for these events.

"Look what Terry Fox did. He was just a boy who got cancer. Instead of letting it get him down, he decided to spread hope. I doubt that a lot of people would have done what he did. I'm sure it wasn't a gift for him to get cancer, but through the research dollars raised from his Marathon's of Hope a lot of lives have been saved!" I said with conviction and passion.

I still remember going to see Terry Fox run through my home town in Oakville over 25 years ago...my mind drifted back in time and for a moment I forgot I was in the playroom talking to Kelly.

"Please Col, as normal as possible. You have to promise me" I pleaded from the phone in the hospital hallway. "I'm not ready to put a damper on the weekend for Ryan and Ella when I don't even have the results yet. We should know in a day or two. I don't want Ryan's 9th Birthday ruined, and Ella is so excited about her Confirmation. I want them distracted." I said, thinking how much I needed to rely on her at this time and was asking a lot of her to pretend, and help plan a party for the kids with Danny's family coming too.

"Share, OK, you know it. Status quo is that what you want?" She asked sounding like she was just as relieved to be able to pretend awhile longer as well. "I'll bring the meats for sandwiches. Don't worry, just take care. How's Colleen?"

"She's good. I'm pretending with her too. Trying to not talk about what's going on but distract ourselves in activity. She's met a friend, her name's Ashley and they are sharing a room now. When

I left to make this call they were blowing bubbles at each other from their beds." I said actually amazed at the smile that was turning up the corner of my mouth. "Please call Pam for me and see if she and anyone else want to go too. Remind everyone, it's going to be a happy time for the kids."

"Sorry Sharon, what did you say?" Kelly pulled me back from my day-dreaming. I had been thinking of the conversation I had had with my sister awhile ago

"Oh, I was just saying how brave Terry Fox was. You know, forget I made any connection between cancer and gifts. I'm with you, it doesn't come wrapped in a bow it comes at you head on like a train wreck." I said, starting to get up from the couch.

Colleen's IV pole was beeping and I needed to call the nurse to the playroom. It would take awhile until I understood why she would be beeping and what I could do about it and not bother the already stretched nursing staff on the seemingly busier childhood Oncology floor. Children weren't supposed to get cancer, but there were just so many. And even in the short space of six days we were there full time, there were so many new kids.

I asked one of the oncologists if it was always this busy and they said that usually there is a steady stream, but some times of the year are busier than others, and we are in our busy time now.

"With the warmer weather the bugs and viruses are all out. The kids taking chemo usually pick up everything. We have noticed that new kids get cancer in waves and some months are busier than others" explained Dr. Chris as best as she could to satisfy my curiosity without going into too much depth.

Was ignorance bliss?

I had never thought that there was a connection between cancer and viruses. She never came out and said it but I did some research after our conversation. I learned that there was some research on the internet done about the Epstein Barr Virus and Colleen's cancer.

I also learned later that Colleen had been tested for this virus when she first came in and tested positive.

This virus is responsible for mononucleosis among other things. Do some kids get cancer and others get mono?

Wasn't this virus already in all the schools? What was the big deal these days about flu shots? I never had them as a child.

Was it coincidental that they now had a chicken pox vaccine? Colleen's health problems seemed to start with the chicken pox!

One of the hundreds of doctors we saw initially was actually doing a study on this connection. I never got her name and have not gone back to seek her results. What's the point? It won't change things for Colleen. Better to keep on going and deal with what's on the plate than worry about what could have been.

If there is a connection I am sure that there are very qualified people working hard on the problem.

"I've got it" said a gentle voice from behind me. "I've already called the nurse" she said moving towards the IV Pole.

She was in her early twenties. She had long brown hair, a warm smile, a gentle and soothing demeanor and wearing a badge that said "Volunteer".

"Hi, I'm still new to this. Thanks for your help" I said grateful for a helping hand. "Are you a child-life specialist trainee?" I asked trying to figure out what she was doing in the playroom on the oncology floor in the middle of the afternoon during the week.

I could see that she was a volunteer, but I guess I was just shocked at there being volunteers in the playroom who were so young. I had seen some older volunteers over the last few days whom I assumed were retired and so could afford the time to help the hospital.

"No, I just wanted to volunteer here. I'm in my final year of university. I love the kids and I think it's an important place to volunteer at a Children's Hospital" She explained with compassion.

I could tell that she really meant what she was saying and her dedication warmed my heart. I was to learn that she would be only one of the many younger volunteers who spread so much joy to the children.

Volunteers are always in short supply, especially dedicated volunteers. We are always so busy, and it really takes little time to volunteer and do something good for someone else to brighten their day and lighten their loads a little.

"Well, I think you're doing a great job, thanks again" Just then a nurse came into the room and approached Kelly. Another nurse came to check the fluids on Colleen's IV pole.

"Kelly, we need to get Ashley back to the room now. The doctors are coming and they want to talk to you about some more tests for Ashley." Said a nurse assigned to Ashley that day.

Each child had their own dedicated nurse each day and night. It was usually not the same person from day to day because while we may have been living in hospital limbo, they actually had lives and time off.

"Come on, Ashley," Kelly said, and helped her up from the table and collected her crafts.

"I'll give you some privacy Kelly, let me know when it's safe to come back," I said as she was leaving. As I said, we were sharing a room for the days leading up to both our children's diagnoses. We became close then, as the four of us all slept in the same room.

She had her chair cot by Ashley's bed, mine was by Colleen's. I learned very quickly in the ensuing days that having roomies you got along with was very comforting and peaceful. Also, the age and interaction between the children was important. The hospital did what they could to match up the children with kids their own age.

Sometimes you would be spending an entire week with another family in a room while your child was being treated, and it was good if everyone got along or had similar parenting styles. It was unpleasant if the children acted up too often despite their illness. Some parents would make no attempts to quiet them down and so it was difficult for anyone to get any sleep.

Also, sometimes other parents had different ways of interacting with the hospital staff. It was hard to witness some of the verbal exchanges that happened between some parents and the doctors. Emotions are stretched beyond bounds and tempers can fly when it comes to looking out for our children.

One of the most difficult things to come to terms with is that in order for the doctors to make our children better they must make them very sick first with the chemo and radiation. I remember talking with Dr. Klassen after Colleen's treatments started.

He seemed very sad. He told me that it was him that was making Colleen so sick by trying to kill her cancer. I can't imagine what it would be like to be in this position and how strong you need to be in your convictions that in the end it will all work out for the best.

"Colleen, honey, finish up your drawing, it's time to go back to your room soon." I said preparing her to leave. Kelly had just come back and told me it was safe to come back to the room.

"OK, Mommy," she said. I looked at her in this environment and thought about what she was missing at home. The end of Grade 1 was all. I had overheard conversations between other parents and I was curious how they were managing their kids' schooling with so much time spent in the hospital.

We tried to stay busy for the rest of the day. I would order dinner for her, play games, and make crafts to help pass the time.

The playrooms often had evening activities planned. I felt like I was in camp as I scanned the schedules taped to their doors.

I was amazed at this whole new world inside the Children's Hospital. I was like most parents up until this point. If you came to the hospital with your child you were usually here for a few hours and then you could go home.

These programs were designed for the families who had to stay for an undetermined amount of time. We were the overnight club. The child-life workers and their volunteers made up these programs and gave a lot of their free time. I wonder if they know how truly helpful they are to parents? How much joy they bring to the kids? How much more bearable it is to be in hospital?

Some floors would have a social night and call kids from other floors in the hospital. I remember once going up to the 5th floor and watching a movie there called *Daddy Daycare.*

The staff and volunteers had made popcorn and had juice for the kids all gathered around the VCR. It looked like one big slumber party except for the fact that most of the kids were attached to IV's receiving some form of treatment. Despite the constant beeping from the IV's it was a very memorable evening for me.

About 9:00 p.m. I would put her to bed. I would quietly leave the room for a few moments and call home. Around 10:00 p.m. I would be tucked into my chair cot in the dark room trying to keep the volume down on the TV in her room.

The night nurse would walk in and out all night long monitoring Colleen's vitals and taking her temperature. Sometimes I would be too upset to sleep so they would take a minute to talk and to reassure you. Eventually sleep would come, and with sleep more nightmares.

We were in limbo until she had a diagnosis of cancer. There were support staff that would stop by, but they all seemed to be waiting in the wings until they knew Colleen had cancer for sure.

The very next day we got our exclusive membership into the childhood cancer club and were introduced to all sorts of new things like home-schooling and the Children's Wish Foundation.

No parent that walks the oncology floor will ever be the same again.

DIAGNOSIS DAY MAY 28, 2003

"Danny, the doctors were by this morning and we have a meeting very soon in the back room" I said as he entered Colleen's room shortly after arriving from work. He had got off early and was carrying his overnight bag to stay the night. I had been at the hospital for six nights straight and I needed a break and wanted to go home and see the other kids.

Danny's family was there now too, and I wanted to try to make a few plans for the weekend's confirmation and birthday party. I had finally resigned myself to the fact that I wouldn't be home.

"Hi Daddy!" Colleen said from her bed, so excited to see him. "They have Pokemon and all sorts of video games to play" she said thrilled to be spending some time with him. Danny had been back and forth but had not stayed overnight yet.

"Sounds great, Sweetie, I'm happy to see you're feeling good," he said casting me a worried glance. Her lymph nodes were still so swollen in her neck, her belly seemed more bloated, and her rash was even darker and more pronounced. "I see we have some good movies to choose from too".

Some kids that got cancer didn't "look" sick all the time. In Colleen's case she looked sick but didn't act sick. Ashley, for example, had a solid tumor on her liver and kidney that was not visible, so outwardly, despite being a little thin, she looked normal. But Ashley had a lot of pain and so at times acted sick. Go figure.

Also, for some kids it's not the cancer that makes them sick but the treatments. The unfortunate reality is that eventually the cancer will affect all the kids if it's left untreated for too long so they will all look and act sick at some point in time. This can happen if they relapse and the chemo stops working for them and there are no other options available.

Later that day…

It was a long narrow passageway and at the end of it was a door. We were being ushered by two people in long white coats who tried not to make eye contact with us and kept their backs to us. I felt as if with each step I took closer to the door I would be forever changed and my life and the lives of my family would be over. Thank goodness I had Danny to hold onto or I may have fallen or decided to run the other way to escape the dread I knew lay waiting for me up ahead.

My eyes were playing tricks on me. It looked as if the door to the room had just opened on its own like you see in horror movies. It looked so dark in the room and I wondered who or what was waiting for us inside. The two people who ushered us to the room were part of the oncology team that would be overseeing Colleen's treatment. They walked in first and motioned for us to follow.

Gathering our courage we entered the room. It looked like a meeting room on the outside, but underneath I sensed that the room had an agenda of its own. I wondered how many parents have made this same walk down the hallway and into this room before us. This room had a feeling of dread and it was sparsely furnished so as not to be too distracting while you were given the bad news. In the middle there was a big rectangular table where a few more doctors sat. They weren't smiling. They nodded their heads and asked us to sit down in one of the empty seats.

There were all sorts of papers in front of each of them and I wondered what they were all about. I knew though. They had the answers, the results were in, and it was now time to act. Was it me, or was there a look of eager anticipation on their faces slightly below their obvious sympathetic outwardly appearance? How could they be excited about this moment? Everything was going to change now and, even though I wanted some answers, I was terrified of what they were going to say.

As I listened to what they said the room started to swim in and out of focus. I felt myself being lifted from my seat by many hands and pulled in different directions. Where was Danny? I couldn't see him anymore and all I could hear now was a terrible loud buzzing in my ears. I heard a scream from down the hall and thought it sounded like Colleen.

"I'm coming Colleen, hold on, I'm going to get you and take you away from here. It's all a terrible mistake and I know if we leave now it will all go away...."

"Sharon! Sharon! Shhh, wake up, you're having a bad dream, you were really upset, are you OK?" It was my sister-in-saw, Trish. Cold sweat trickled down my forehead and I struggled to adjust my eyes. Her hands were on my shoulders trying to settle me down. I was dreaming and her hands were what I was feeling in my dream.

"Huh?" I said as my vision cleared and I realized where I was. "Sorry, I was just dreaming about earlier today." I had fallen asleep on the coach in my living room after being exhausted from retelling what had happened at the hospital earlier in the day and decisions Danny and I would have to make regarding Colleen's health.

"I don't know what to say, I could never imagine having to decide something like this, and I can't even pretend to know what you must be going through," she said as she stood up and moved to a chair to sit down. "It's not fair and no parent or child should have to go through this!"

As tears started to cloud my eyes and I struggled to keep them down, I realized what an important decision that needed to be made overnight and I had no idea what I was going to do. My head said one thing, my heart said another. I needed some input from my family to help me think.

"So, is it common to get a lot of side effects from the chemo?" Asked Trish trying to keep her own voice steady. I could tell she was trying to be brave and was doing her best to stay relaxed.

"Well, as you can see by this information they gave us that outlines all the possible side effects from the chemo, it must be pretty common." I said as I started to flip through the pages. "Heart damage, brain damage, brittle bones, vomiting, hair loss, liver damage, pain, bowel and intestine problems, infertility, oh and I like this one the best, growth problems." I said flipping page to page through the different side effects for the different drugs. "I don't think Colleen will have a problem there considering the size of her now and her current genes," I said trying to add some humour to the dismal possibilities. "And the papers say there are no guarantees about whether it will work and what will be left of her after the treatment is over. She could still die after having to go through all this!"

"Well, are there any other options at all? What about herbal remedies. I know someone who is cancer free because they chose an alternative route than chemo," she said trying as best as she could to be positive.

"I don't know. They say that her cancer is very advanced and very aggressive and she needs to start right away. They gave us this "protocol," which is basically a road map for the next two years based on research that was done with other children across the world who have the same cancer as Colleen."

"Two years of chemo everyday?" She said in astonishment.

"I didn't think people took chemo that long either, but it's true. Her cancer is everywhere in her body" I said "They say that she gets stronger stuff at first, then as time goes on she gets less and less."

"Do all the kids get the same treatments?'

"No, it depends on their type of cancer and how far it's spread, apparently. Her treatment will be determined by a computer. She qualifies to take part in a clinical trial. Her name goes into the computer and it randomly selects one of four treatment plans for her type of cancer."

"What? Don't the doctors decide?" She asked obviously confused with the process. I wasn't an expert either but I had listened intently earlier to the doctors when they presented our options.

"They said that she could have the standard therapy and dosage if we chose not to participate in this "clinical trial." It's a randomized blind study and the computer assigns the treatment plan. At the end of the treatment the doctors can compare which kids did better on what treatments. Some are much worse than others and it's a matter of chance which one you get."

"What's a clinical trial?" She asked really trying to follow what I was saying.

"It's like a science experiment. There is a standard amount of chemo they have given in the past to kids with this cancer. But it didn't seem to work well for the ones who were in the late stages of the disease when they were diagnosed like Colleen. So the Oncologists are trying stronger dosages and different medicines to see if it will be better and then will compare the results."

I couldn't believe I was talking so calmly about this now. Earlier at the hospital I had been so upset that I wouldn't sign the papers right away. I told the doctors I needed time to read the side effects and decide if I wanted Colleen to have experimental treatment selected for her by a random computer selection. I was reluctant to play Russian roulette with my daughter's life!

"I think you may be the first parent to want to consider this overnight," said Dr. Halton; one of the Oncologists at the table.

She was a very professional lady who seemed to really know her stuff. I could tell that she was concerned about Colleen and wanted to start her treatment right away. Danny was supportive of waiting too and so we agreed that when I came back the next day we would decide.

On the way home in the car I wondered how many other children had died in order to produce this "protocol" for the clinical trial. Obviously some kids must have suffered terrible side effects from the treatments or how else would they have been able to list them as possibilities?

Where did they get the numbers to predict prognosis if not for the fact that they simply added up who lived and who died? A terrible thought so intense invaded my mind I almost drove off the road. Colleen would just be another statistic. How well she did, or how poorly she did would be recorded and kept in files that could be accessed by doctors all over the world. Where was my little girl in all of this?

I could see them entering information on her progress into their computers in my mind's eye. She was a person, but they would only see numbers and outcomes. Any reactions she had to medications, any side effects suffered, would all be recorded and results tabulated.

Then all of this information on Colleen would help build new protocols that would become standard therapy for other children. All of this was too overwhelming to consider. Is this what happened? Was cancer treatment all about learning from the mistakes of the past? How do you define mistake, what were their names? Where did they live? What happened to their families? No, I said to myself. This can't be.

What if we got the wrong treatment and she ended up being a mistake from which others would learn from? The mistake was the fact she got cancer in the first place. The standard treatment was safer. But was it only safer in the short run? I was driving myself crazy as I imagined all sorts of terrible outcomes. What if she did well, how many lives would she save?

As I was turning onto my street I had worked myself into such a state I had to pull over before getting to the house. I must have spent five minutes hysterically bawling my eyes out in the car. I remember screaming at the top of my lungs about the injustice of this all. I managed to calm myself down by telling myself that Colleen was now in God's hands, and to trust that whatever happened to her would be fine.

"Just promise me that if you intend to take her one day that you won't let her suffer now!" I pleaded staring straight into the sky.

To this day, and with all of our hurdles, I can honestly say He's been good to His word. I remembered how my mom and sister had suffered by living longer. They were both very active women and in the end were reduced to paralysis, immobility, and a lot of pain as side effects. I didn't want to see this for my six year old child if she was to live longer and get over this.

The word "hope" was taking on a whole new meaning for me as I struggled to find something to cling onto that would help me through the day. It would be two years before we knew if the "hope" they offered us then with the "clinical trial" would actually transpire.

All we had now was an experimental treatment plan, uncertainty and no guarantees. Would she live or would she die? And if she lived, what would be left of the little girl I have now at the end?

"You want something to eat Share?" I heard my sister Colleen in the kitchen. She was working so hard to keep everything normal as I had asked.

"I'm not hungry, thanks, come in here with Trish, I want you to hear this more and give me some feedback." I asked, knowing that she would offer whatever insight she could, but knowing she would have started the treatment already.

She rushed into things quicker than me sometimes. I knew she wouldn't have hesitated to sign and ask questions later if it had been her daughter.

Earlier in the day at our Meeting:

"Don't take too long," Dr. Klassen said after Dr. Halton had left the room and basically said the same thing. "We should get started right away; time is very important." I understood his sense of urgency, but we had already waited over eight days, what was another 12 hours?

"Tomorrow I'll be back. I'm going home overnight for some rest. I need to feel like I've read and understand everything." I said as the doctors started gathering their papers and prepared to leave.

"OK, but we'll have to start something tomorrow." He said in such a way as to make me feel like I was losing control of her care now that her diagnosis was known. Decisions regarding her health and well-being were now in the hands of this team of Oncologists!

I had to keep reminding myself that they were not the enemy

but our allies in this battle against cancer.

As it turned out, my initial feelings of losing control of our lives was very real. For the next two years they called the shots. They told us what to do and not to do, and when to do it.

We were kept on a short leash and couldn't venture too far away from the hospital in case we had to rush her in at their command.

They said that once we started this treatment plan, there was no turning back. We had to go the whole way regardless of how she reacted or what happened to her.

For the next two years we were to be slaves to this protocol, the thermometer, and the whims of these doctors. That's why I knew they wanted us to sign in advance of starting, I'm sure if things go wrong, a lot of parents want to back out and stop.

There were no options as far as missing appointments either. Sometimes they would be flexible, but usually they made you stick to the treatment plan.

Everything was about timing and intensity of treatments and to deviate would skew the results. So forget about any plans you may have made for the future before she was diagnosed.

We were told that when the treatment started that she would likely be in hospital for up to six weeks before she could go home.

She would be taken out of school for the rest of the year, and assigned some in-hospital tutoring to finish Grade 1.

They told us that we would be connected with Marilyn, an Interlink nurse who would "when things settled down" come for a "home visit" to discuss what services were available and discuss home-schooling for Grade 2.

They said she would be too sick to go to school and would be spending a lot of time at the hospital getting treatments that it wouldn't be possible to do anything else. The chemo was killing her immune system and without an immune system she could die if she got too sick. She couldn't be around too many people for a long time.

They assigned a social worker to our family and made some other suggestions about the support that was available in the hospital.

Thinking back to the way I felt then, and what they were able to do for Colleen, I am so grateful to them for saving her life. I know that they have to be firm because so much can go wrong and they try to control what they can. It just takes awhile to get used to not having freedom and being at the mercy of someone else for your child's life.

"I know they are only thinking of Colleen's welfare, they're good doctors and I know they are there to help," I said trying to convince myself that we should go ahead with it. "Our society may have alternatives to chemo, but the statistics are based on medical remedies, not herbal ones." I had just gone over in my head what had played out after the meeting earlier in the day and I was starting to come to a decision.

"What happens after two years?" Asked Trish, "Is she all better and that's it. No more hospital?" I looked at her and realized that I didn't know the answer. Was it possible that we would put in our time, do what we needed to do, and she would miraculously be cured?

"Oh no, there is an after-care clinic at the Children's Hospital that will monitor her health until she's 18 and then she will go to a clinic at the General Hospital." I said. Part of me was very doubtful that she would ever get through this treatment plan considering the fact that cancer had already won the battle in my family by taking my parents and my oldest sister already.

Cancer was cruel and unpredictable. It had invaded my innocent baby so young, how could she possibly live being infected so young? Her cancer was one of the most aggressive ones to get. It was harder to treat than Leukemia. Kids died from Leukemia all the time, didn't they? At least that's what I thought before any of this happened to us.

"Well, that sounds positive," she said, "she'll be well looked after" she finished trying to force a smile.

"Yeah" I thought. She'll be looked after all right. In the stuff they gave me to read it said that there was a strong chance the cancer would come back in another part of her body. It said that sometimes the treatment was so toxic that a different cancer could come back in her organs. It also said that with her cancer there was a strong chance it would come back in her brain.

They weren't monitoring to see how she was, as much as monitoring her for a relapse. They knew it would happen, just not when and where it would strike again. And they also wanted to keep track of all the damage the drugs did to her body for their clinical trial and to adjust things for other children after her.

Would she have learning disabilities? Would her kidneys fail and she need dialysis for the rest of her life? Would she need a liver transplant? Would she lose her hearing or go blind? Would she end up in a wheelchair because she's had a stroke that's rendered her paralyzed like some of the kids I knew whose hearts were damaged from the drugs that saved their lives? Would she have children?

Then they could enter these statistics into their little computers as time went on. It occurred to me as I was considering all of this that the kids were Guinea pigs. Except they were children, not pigs...they were GUINEA KIDS! They were test subjects and these doctors were mad scientists! They were using our kids as EXPERIMENTS!

Whoa, Sharon, I said to myself. I was heading into negative thinking territory and it wasn't doing any good, it was lunacy. I've always had an actively graphic imagination, and now it needed to calm down a little and be rational if I was going to make the right decision. They weren't mad scientists and Colleen wasn't an experiment. They didn't give her the cancer, it wasn't their fault. They are healers, and they were trying to give us hope. They were trying to save her.

They couldn't tell us if it would work or not, or whether something would go wrong along the way. They weren't gods. Of course they are going to monitor her for the rest of her life. I should be grateful she's in such good hands and receiving such good care. How could I think negatively of this? Our whole society and medical field is based on statistics.

We're all statistics in one way or another. We lead our lives and make choices. The lifestyle choices we make will give us a percentage of whether we will get this condition or that condition. In school there are statistics that measure intelligence and success of programs. At work there are statistics for productivity and profit based on an employee's education, commitment, and loyalty.

So many more things are monitored in everyone's lives. Don't we go to a dentist so they can monitor the health of our teeth and put in fillings when we eat too much candy? Doesn't an optometrist monitor the health of our eyes? I was starting to get a grip and come to terms with what needed to be done.

What if Colleen did really well and her statistics were good? What if what she went through and actually helped saved the life of another child? I liked this thinking a lot better and I vowed to keep this positive thought in my head as we moved forward over the next few days.

"Ella and Ryan are asleep," said Maureen, my other sister-in-law, who was visiting to help out. She had just tucked them in and was coming to join us.

Maureen had lost her own father to cancer when her first child was born. She named him after her father. She also had two blind children of her own. Fate had certainly dealt her a full plate. She would say "God never gives you more than he knows you can handle". Well, she certainly had earned the right to say that in my eyes and I was able to take strength from her calm presence and reassuring words.

The rest of the evening went by with five women trying not to focus on what decisions Danny and I would make, but making plans for the upcoming party on the weekend. There were moments that I would not be able to pretend and simply break down in wrenching sobs, but they passed, and eventually it was time for bed.

When the party came a few days later everyone did a terrific job. I saw the pictures and Ella and Ryan looked happy and thoroughly spoiled. Colleen and I were in an isolation room when the big day had came and she was starting to get sick from the chemo. I'll never forget the feeling of helplessness that day, and rage, and anger, and I'll never forget how lucky I am to have such a wonderful family.

MAY 29, 2003, Day 1 - CHEMO

I arrived by 10:00 a.m. at the hospital. Danny was in the room with Colleen playing a video game. The doctors were due to arrive soon for rounds.

"Well, how was the night?" I asked him knowing full well that his six-foot four frame and 260 lbs would have had a difficult night on the convertible chair-cot.

"It was great. We played games and watched movies and Colleen and I got a chance to make these bracelets." He picked them up off the side table in the room. He would need to get to work soon, and it was a new job, and a busy time. And we needed his job.

We went out into the hallway to have a private conversation.

"Well?" I asked him in a hushed voice "What do you want to

do?" I had already come to terms that we should sign the papers but I wanted his opinion too.

"I think we should. I talked to a parent last night who said that their child was having no problems with the chemo, and that aside from their hair falling out, was actually doing great"

"Yeah, but what kind of cancer do they have and how aggressive are the treatments?" I said in an accusatory tone, "that makes a big difference". Oh oh, Mrs. Negativity creeping back again into my head.

"Look Sharon, what choice do we have? Colleen's a strong girl. She can get through this. She's got our strength too. It's not as if taking care of people going through chemo will be new to us," he said trying to calm in me what he could see as rising panic. "I was there with my dad, and your family, we are slightly more experienced than most people here".

"I know!" I said now starting to cry. "That's what gets to me. They're all dead!"

"You can't think like that. Colleen's different. It's our only hope. Think what will happen if we don't do anything. Will you be able to live with yourself?" He asked knowing he was getting through to me. I had already decided to do it but it was comforting to hear how positive he was too.

It would have been horrible if I had made the decision on my own and something happened. We were in this together now and, as an entire family, including Ella and Ryan at home and everyone else.

There was no more time to talk, the doctors were coming. I could see the expectant looks on their faces as they were eager to start treating Colleen. Before they could ask, I said "We signed the papers, let's hope this works," I said trying as best I could to reflect in my expression one of joy and happiness. "What's next?"

They told us that they would need to put in a port-o-catheter soon that would be surgically implanted attached to her main arteries to facilitate the extraction of blood and the infusions of chemo. They would be checking with the surgeon to see how soon this could be done.

They said that a nurse would be by shortly to give her her first dose. They asked if someone had talked to us about being a direct blood donor to Colleen. She was going to need a lot of blood soon to replace the blood that would be destroyed by the medicine. Danny and I both showed interest in doing this but they cautioned us about being too optimistic.

"A lot of parents want to do this. In truth, it would take more blood than you or your husband has in your body to get her through this," he said with a sad tone to his voice. "We think it's important for the kids to have some of the parents' blood, it's not scientifically proven that it works better than other people's blood, but it seems to help the parent feel like they are contributing in some way."

"Both of us can give her blood, right?" I asked hoping the answer would be yes.

"Usually only one parent is compatible with the child" he said wondering which of us would be. My husband is a strong man with a lot of iron in his blood. If he had to choose one of us I bet he would have chosen him. Unfortunately it's not a matter of choice, only blood type.

"I'm O negative," said my husband. "I'm a universal donor. I can give blood to anyone". That's right! I thought, hopefully this was a good sign of things to come because I was pretty sure that I was compatible with her already.

"Well, I'll let the nurse know and she can tell you both where to go to get tested. Let me caution you, not everyone can give blood."

Oh, oh, I thought, here's the catch. "It's not your fault if you can't and you can't let it get you down."

"What do you mean?" I asked starting to worry that we wouldn't be able to do it.

"There's a lot of screening done these days for blood donors. We don't want to pass on any tainted blood to the children."

"What do you mean by tainted blood? Do you mean like Hepatitis B and West Nile?" I asked wanting to know what he meant.

"Exactly, those viruses and many more things found in blood. We'll keep our fingers crossed that you can both donate" he said and left the room.

"Well, what do you think, Danny?"

"Let's go get tested," he said and we waited for the instructions from the nurse.

Being a Direct Donor

"What an eye opener!" I said to my husband a few days later. "Can you believe what happened? It's a darn good thing we have led a relatively boring life so far"

We took turns going to the blood donor clinic in the city to donate. Every time you went it was the same routine. You went into a room with a nurse who had a long sheet of paper full of questions that you had to answer yes or no to.

"These questions are very important to determine if you can give blood to Colleen. Even though you are a match, you may have contracted something and don't know it."

"Wouldn't I know?" I asked confused.

"No, sometimes things like West Nile have no symptoms at all. You could be a carrier of a lot of other things and not know it.

"OK, makes sense, I guess" I wondered what other things could go undetected in your blood and you not know it? I got my answer when she started to ask personal questions about sexual behavior and intravenous drug use. I was shocked to hear that if you had traveled to certain places in the World recently that this might also hinder you from donating.

"OK, that's it, now we need to go into the clinic to draw your blood then take it over to the lab at CHEO," she said as she finished the paperwork in front of her.

"What are those bar codes for?" I asked as she pulled a set out of her drawer.

"Well, the questions I've asked you are very personal. Sometimes it's embarrassing to tell the truth to a live person."

"I agree completely, those are personal questions. I'll know if Danny has kept any secrets from me if for some reason he can't donate to Colleen," I said with a little bit of a chuckle in my voice.

"Don't laugh, sometimes it happens, but this blood is going to your child, it needs to be pure. People need to leave marital issues out of the equation."

"So what are the bar codes for?" I asked secretly hoping that I wouldn't get any surprises from my husband of almost 20 years.

"I'm going to leave the room now. We will draw your blood and put it in this plastic bag. There is a YES bar code and a NO bar code, see here on the label?"

"Yes, I can see the different answers."

"I won't know how you answer because there will only be the bar code on the bag. If, for some reason you think that you shouldn't donate your blood to Colleen, or that perhaps you weren't all that truthful in your answers, put the NO bar code on the bag. On the other hand if you feel confident and want her to have your blood, put the YES bar code on the bag."

"Who reads the bar codes?" I asked completely astonished at the process.

"After we've taken your blood we send it to the lab who then scans the bar code. If you answered NO, they simply dispose of your blood."

"So if you weren't truthful, you still have to give your blood anyway?" I asked, thinking that you really needed to be sure of yourself before coming here or this whole experience could be very embarrassing.

"No, a person could get up and leave. You can change your mind at any time without explanation.

It turned out that both Danny and I were acceptable donors and we both answered YES on our bags which meant for me that we didn't have any secrets. Danny donated the first batch of blood, and then I went after him.

We continued like this for a long while. He would go one week and I the next. We needed to rest in between or we would have become too weak. At one point Colleen needed so much blood there would have been no way for us to be her exclusive donors.

The chemo was killing all of her blood cells, not only the cancerous ones. She needed red blood cells as well as platelet transfusions almost daily for awhile. I found out that they had matched Colleen up with someone in Ottawa who was a platelet donor. I call them angels.

Platelets take longer to harvest than regular blood cells. It takes almost three hours hooked up to a machine for one dose. I would look over at the platelet donors when I went to donate. A lot of them were businessmen. They sat in big comfortable chairs and while their platelets were harvested they could plug into the internet, watch TV, or talk on cell phones.

"Do you normally have to match the kids up to a donor?" I asked the nurse who was just attaching a bag of platelets to Colleen's IV Pole to be infused right away.

"Well, they need to be a match most of all. But the truth is sometimes even the matched donor can't keep up with demand from the child they are saving. Then it's up to us nurses to get on the phone and see if we can track down some platelets at another hospital," she said opening the valve so the transfusion could start.

Colleen was sitting quietly in the bed completely absorbed in her movie and oblivious to the fact that without this transfusion she could have bled to death internally because she had zero platelets in her body.

"This is another world in here isn't it? You nurses are really important and save lives everyday with a simple phone call. Thanks for finding this blood for her." I said stifling tears that threatened to burst forth in torrents of gratitude.

"Managed to find this blood in Saskatchewan today and had it flown in for Colleen. I'm really glad it's finally here. There's no other blood in Ottawa and our local donors are tapped out. This was the closest place that had a match for Colleen." She said getting ready to take a blood pressure reading on Colleen to make sure she wasn't having a reaction to the transfusion. The kids had to be monitored so closely because some children have had severe complications from this process.

"It makes it really hit home about being a blood donor and giving the gift of life. I wonder if people really know how much they are doing when they decide to donate."

"I think that the ones that donate have a pretty good idea how important it is. It's trying to get the rest of the people to understand." She said and then went on to check Colleen's temperature. Colleen's movie was coming to an end and she didn't like the constant interruptions by the nurse.

"You just took my temperature a minute ago," she said defiantly.

"I know, Sweetie, but until we're done, I'm going to be bothering you a lot more." I chuckled at how easily and calm this nurse was to both administer a life-saving blood transfusion and banter back and forth with an impatient six year old.

I'll never forget one day for the rest of my life:

Colleen was about two months into her treatments now and we were headed into the hospital to be admitted for five days and countless rounds of chemo. These admissions were well laid out in our protocol so at least there was some ability to plan where you would be and when.

I had wanted to stop in at the blood donor clinic to give because she was fresh out of our blood and I knew she would need some by the end of the week. I introduced her to the nurse who ran down the usual set of questions before settling me into the big chair and inserting the needle.

She sat in a chair across from me and watched as my blood was being pumped into a bag by a big machine.

"Does it hurt, Mommy?" She asked concerned.

"Not at all," I said. "Besides, you are the queen of needles and never complain, it wouldn't look good if I complained about getting needles only sometimes?" I said thinking that not a lot of people can lay claim to this experience and I'm sure given the choice, would never want to.

"Just think baby, they are taking my blood here, then they will drive this bag over to CHEO, and then they will hook it up and put it straight into you." I said trying to make this whole experience sound fun and exciting and different.

In truth I was feeling a little surreal about the whole thing and couldn't believe it was happening. What happened to before she got sick and the only thing we passed back and forth were flu bugs?

"Daddy's blood feels different from yours sometimes. I get this funny taste in my mouth." She said trying to explain how she felt.

"Does this really happen?" I asked her not believing that this was possible to taste blood being transfused. "Does it happen with my blood?"

"Not all the time, but mostly your blood makes me feel warm inside," she said and it was all I could do not to break down into tears. Maybe she tasted all the iron in Danny's blood?

Later in the week when her hemoglobin dropped way below normal levels as a result of the chemo, I was relieved to know that we had taken a short detour on our way in. It was such a good feeling to hear the doctor cry out, "Mom's blood is in the building, let's call it up right away and get it transfused!"

In hindsight our efforts to become direct donors really paid off all around. I'm sure that the hospital staff was relieved as well. There are so many children in need of blood in every hospital across Canada.

Our blood takes a little pressure off of demand and helps increase the supply to others in need.

AND SO IT WENT....UNTIL MAY 24, 2005

July 2003

The little pre-diagnosis routine I had established was quickly disrupted once the chemo started. At times when she could have gone for the morning playgroup she was getting a spinal tap. In the afternoon she was tired from the medicine and so would sleep.

"We can't go to the playroom today, baby; your counts are too low. But Brenda's sending over a volunteer with some crafts for you to do in the room. How does that sound?" I asked her as she looked at me miserably.

She had this strange rash all over her body and she was also running a terribly high fever.

"OK, I guess. When will I be better?" She asked. She was always asking me when she would get better. If something was taken away, or her movements were restricted, she always asked me when things would go back to normal.

I had nothing to say other than: "Soon, Honey, after this next transfusion your counts should come up and then we can go to the playroom and maybe even be able to go home," I said with every ounce of energy I had to force a smile.

The truth is we were spending way too much time in isolation and it was wearing both of our spirits down.

We had been told by Dr. Klassen recently that all of Colleen's lymph nodes were shrunk thanks to the high dose Prednisone, and it was nothing short of a miracle that she had responded as well as she did to the chemo.

Unfortunately, a few days later she had a rash appear on her skin. They thought it was chicken pox and so stopped her chemo and put us in isolation pending the results of a test that would provide conclusive proof. Chicken pox can be fatal to people with no immunity and the chemo was lowering her immune system.

The doctors and nurses had to follow strict rules when coming into our room. They had to put on gloves, masks and gowns at the door. I felt like we were in quarantine. It was not a good feeling.

After a few days of watching the strange rash change form and move all over her body I insisted that it was not the Chicken Pox, but that the lymphoma was back.

"That's not realistic," said Dr. Klassen to me. "She responded well to the initial therapy."

"Well, my theory is that it's still in her skin and unless we start the chemo right away to kill it, things will get worse!" I wasn't being complacent anymore and I was learning to trust my instincts. I was also feeling confined and a little impatient.

He finally relented and did a biopsy of one of the spots on her arm. She still has the scar. It came back positive for lymphoma. If I hadn't have been so upset at learning that the cancer was still alive, I might have said, "I told you so."

The doctor started the chemo right away, and within days the rash was gone and we were let out of isolation.

"How's Ashley doing?" I asked Kelly. We were lucky enough to be sharing a room after Colleen and I got out of isolation. Ashley and Kelly had been hospitalized full time since the end of May.

Ashley's tests had come back positive for cancer as well. She had the same late-stage Non-Hodgkin's Lymphoma as Colleen, very rare and very invasive, called Burkett's Lymphoma.

This is a solid tumor that could be operated on as opposed to Colleen's tumors that were spread throughout her lymphatic system.

I remembered clearly back to that day in May when I told Kelly what type and what stage of cancer Colleen had. She had been so sympathetic and very supportive as I told her about the prognosis and treatment.

"Kelly, I pray to God that Ashley's going to be fine. You'll have better news".

"She's OK, I guess. They didn't get all the cancer in the surgery, but they are hoping that with more chemo it will all be killed.' she told me as we shared a sandwich I had just made in the SENS DEN on our floor.

This room was paid for and furnished by our local pro hockey team the Ottawa Senators. I can't describe to you what a blessing this room was. It was like a family living room with a big screen TV and a fridge and microwave. Parents could cook their own meals there, or just go there to talk and be alone.

The girls were watching a movie in the next room so we had decided to take a little break and have a talk. The nurses were keeping an eye out if anything went wrong. They knew we needed to talk.

"How long is Ashley's protocol? Any idea how long you'll have to be in the hospital?" I asked her almost confusing the word hospital with prison. I was still feeling the confines of the isolation room.

"They say that we should be finished within six months."

"That's great news. I wish ours would be over in six months. Colleen's treatments won't be done until 2005! That's a very long time, it's still 2003," I said picturing the long journey ahead in my mind's eye. "I have no idea how we are going to be able to do this?"

"What do you mean?" Asked Kelly not sure what I was talking about.

"Either Danny or myself will need to be there full-time for her. Our protocol expects us in the hospital quite a lot. We've already been here a lot and we seem to be running into a lot of complications." I said feeling a little defeated. "She won't be going to school next year and now I am making plans to arrange for an in-house teacher at home"

"They say that Ashley will probably be able to go to school in the New Year"

"That's terrific. What's Brian doing without you? How's your son at home?"

"Brian is commuting from North Bay and staying in Ronald McDonald House when he can in between work. I haven't seen my son for awhile, but my family is helping out a lot while I'm not there."

"Kelly, what about your job you have? What's happening?" I asked. It was becoming very clear that it was impossible for both parents to work while their kids were undergoing treatment.

"Fortunately my boss has been good about this. He's keeping my job and the girls are filling in. It's a small family-run business and I'm only part-time anyway." She said looking like she really missed being home.

"Are you getting paid while you're off, Kelly?" I asked. Even part-time income was hard to replace if you relied on it for groceries and other small things.

"No, UIC won't pay me because they say that because my child is the one who is sick and not me, that I don't qualify for any type of UIC."

"That doesn't make sense?" I asked, wondering how it could be so stringent.

"Well, I suppose if he laid me off I could get it. But that's not honest and I don't want to put him in any awkward positions. It's against the law", She said with determination. "And I don't want to quit," she said sounding very firm. "The doctors think we'll all be back to normal in a matter of months."

"That's not right. You can get up to a year off on UIC if you've paid for it to bring a new baby into the world, it doesn't make sense that when your child is so sick that you're not allowed to draw any. It's not as if you had any choice in the matter," I said starting to get a little heated at the injustice of it all.

"I know, but it's as if it doesn't matter."

"You have your protocol, and I have mine. We didn't make them up, but we have to follow them or else our children may not survive. We're not exactly on vacation here!" I said a little more forcibly. "I can understand if they won't cover the two-year sentence we have to serve, but they should at least cover your six months!" I said, even angrier.

"I know, but what can we do about it? The lady at the UIC office Brian talked to said there were no exceptions. She was sympathetic and all, but said her hands were tied and rules were rules. What about you, what are you going to do to manage?" She asked, curious about my situation.

"Well, I work in a bank. I'm supposed to supervise six people and work with numbers all day. With what has been happening these last weeks there is no way at all I could focus on my work. I'm a basket case, Kel. I can't eat, I'm having trouble sleeping, and I can't concentrate. I find myself walking in circles in the hallway not sure which way I was heading," I said being totally honest with her.

"Yeah, I have my moments too," she said trying to cheer me up.

What was happening to our family life was horrible. I missed my other kids all the time. Danny and I were strangers that pass in the night.

While I was in the hospital he had to be home with the other kids. Our extended family had long since gone home so it was just us.

He would come one night every week to relieve me so I could go home to see the kids. Then he would come back on Friday night and stay till Sunday while I went home and did things around the house and took a rest.

Sunday mornings I would head back with the kids to the hospital to change over with Danny so he could go to work the next day. They had to wait in the parking lot for their Dad to come out because they still couldn't get into the hospital with the SARS restrictions in place.

I would say goodbye to them all, and would return to the room with Colleen. She was either in an isolation room depending on her counts or a room to share with another family. We settled in Sunday nights and waited to see what the next week would bring.

"So what's happening with your job?" She asked curiously.

"Right now my doctor has signed me off on short-term stress leave. Do you believe that in order to get the paperwork done I had to leave Colleen during one of her lumbar punctures to get the paperwork completed?" I said both relieved at the leave and annoyed that for some reason paperwork had to take precedence over my child.

"How long will you be off?" She asked. I could tell she was thinking about the next two years of treatment we still had.

"I don't know Kel; I'm just going through the motions, trying to be strong for Colleen and trying to think about what we are going to do. Every time I try to come up with a solution something happens, either blood in the urine, or an elevated heart level, or a failing liver, that I have to give up thinking about how we are going to pay our bills and get back to giving all my energy to Colleen" I said sounding more exhausted than I actually felt at that moment.

"Does your husband have any benefits?" She asked.

"Nope, he's in the same boat as you I guess with the UIC. And from what you're telling me there's nothing there either" I said defeated.

"So, I'm hoping to go home soon when we get a break in treatment. It's hard to do all this from the hospital and Danny has no time working full-time and being with the kids. I talked to my boss and he says everything should be OK for a while longer and all he cares about is that Colleen and I are fine." I said, very grateful to have such a good branch manager.

"Does he know that she will need treatment for the next two years?" She asked with a hint of laughter in her voice.

"Well, no, I haven't actually got there yet. One day when it's quiet and we are at home, I'll bring home all this paperwork and show him in person what we're up against. I don't know what to say. I love my job and don't want to lose it either!"

"Someone should tell the government about this. It's not our fault. It's not fair" she said as if she was suggesting that we had to be punished on top of dealing with sick children.

"Anyhow, I'm pretty sure I'm being paid awhile longer. I couldn't work considering all this. I know I would be at my desk and break out crying, I'm sure that would look marvelous to the clients and my staff. I think that for now you could honestly say I am really stressed-out. I just need to get a hold of myself so I can think this through, there has to be a solution." I said praying that I would come up with a miracle solution to a desperate problem.

The thought of leaving my child at this point was completely unbearable and if I had to be separated now I think I'd actually lose my mind. They would have to commit me for sure.

"I overheard another mom talking. At her husband's work a bunch of people offered to give up some of their holiday time and give it to him so he could be with their son. She doesn't work, and he wanted to be here for the treatments." She offered.

"I couldn't do that Kelly. I couldn't take someone's holidays no matter what. How do you think I would feel if something happened in their families and they needed the time but they had given it to me? I would feel awful. Where does this guy work?" I asked wondering what employer allowed this to happen.

"I think she either said the military or the police. It could have been the firefighters though. I'm pretty sure one of those, but don't quote me on it." She said struggling to remember which place it had been. "Maybe it was a high tech company? Oh, I don't know. All I know is that this is what happened," she said, trying to make a point. "Oh, and another mom I talked to said she was in the government and that they were really good about it and giving her all the time she needed."

"What does that mean? Does that mean the government will give her two years off?" I was definitely curious at this point.

"She implied it I guess; I didn't ask her the direct question. Maybe it's shorter than two years. But she did say that they were very good and she was getting paid."

"Really?" I said committing this conversation to what memory was working in my brain. This didn't sound fair and I'm sure there must be more of an explanation.

We then finished our sandwich and headed back to the room as the movie ended.

Chapter Four

"Hello?" I said in a rushed tone into the phone. I was holding a hairbrush full of Colleen's hair that was falling out in clumps in the bathroom. She had gone to the bathroom and was looking in the mirror and started to pull out her own hair. My heart broke. I had seen my mom do the same thing when she lost her hair and now I was watching my six-year-old daughter who was so proud or her hair, doing the same thing. I had taken a hairbrush and was helping her to take out the loose strands.

"Is Sharon Ruth there?" The woman's voice said at the other end of the line.

"Speaking," I said wondering who would be calling and struggling to keep back my tears at what was happening in the bathroom.

"This is Patti, I'm from your bank's insurance company, I'm in charge of your case," she said to me sounding oddly detached.

Did she have any idea what I was doing at the moment? I was trying to be calm. Colleen didn't need me to be weak, she needed me to be strong so we could get through her going bald together.

"Hi. What's up?" I asked as I could feel my heart beat faster and faster. I was starting to panic. I got the feeling this was going to be bad news. I knew I wasn't ready to go back to work yet. I couldn't concentrate and I was not sleeping. I hadn't come to terms with all this and there was no way at all I could keep it together and do my job considering it has only been a few weeks since this all started. Not to mention I was still grieving the loss of my sister to cancer six months earlier.

"I have been looking over your case, and I feel that what you are experiencing is a SEVERE GRIEF REACTION over your daughter's illness and your sister's death. Unfortunately, this does not entitle you to the bank's short-term income protection. I have approved your absence until next week at which time you must return to work or you will not be paid," she said as if reading from a script. "You could apply for a compassionate leave under the bank's program for one year; you won't get paid, but your job will be guaranteed, but not necessarily at the branch you're working at now."

This wasn't happening, it couldn't be. My head started to spin and I was feeling light-headed. I fell down onto my bed and struggled to catch my breath. "I can't go back to work now, I'm not ready, I'm not well", I started to plead into the phone

"This is more than grief!" I now started to cry and hyperventilate. "I need my job and I need to get paid or we'll lose everything," I started to blurt out. "I love my job, but I don't want the people at work to see me this way, I'm no good to anyone." I was running out of steam. "Please don't make me have to go back to work yet," and then I cried, heart wrenching sobs, I let it all out, I shook uncontrollably as I lay on my bed and curled my knees up to my chest. All the while Colleen was still in the bathroom pulling out her hair.

"Oh," she said, a little startled at my reaction, "Maybe I made a mistake," she said sounding now more human than when she first called. "It would appear that you might be suffering from a little depression. Are you all right?" She asked now sounding sympathetic.

"I can't stop crying," I told her as I was also having trouble catching my breath.

"Sharon, is your daughter there with you?" She asked now sounding alarmed.

"Yeees," I managed between gasps.

"You have to calm down, you have to pull yourself together," she said now trying to soothe me enough so I could get control of my emotions. "You have to look after your daughter. Is there someone you can call to help you now?" She asked hoping there was someone who could come over and keep an eye on me.

"Uhuh, my sister is on her way over," I said very grateful that my sister had called and was coming by to see if there was something she could help with. "She'll be here soon."

"Do you feel suicidal, Sharon?" She asked completely throwing me off.

"No, I don't want to kill myself," I said actually mentally considering that if I did all this would be over. "I want to live."

"Good. I'm going to re-open your case. I think that you have more than a grief reaction. I'm going to schedule you an appointment with our independent psychologist who will be able to evaluate you more closely. Depending on those results we can extend your claim longer."

"Thank you so much." I was so relieved that I felt a weight lifting from my neck.

"I'll send you a letter in the mail with the appointment. Don't worry about work. I want you to get better so you can look after your daughter." She said, and with that, hung up.

It turned out I had no trouble at the independent psychologist. He had written and verbal tests and I passed all of them with flying colours. He diagnosed me with agitated depression. With a treatment plan, counseling and proper medication, I would be back to normal in no time.

I was off for four months. My insurance company would only cover me until I started to feel better. I started to take the medication and go for counseling and it was making me stronger emotionally to handle things and come to terms with what was happening with Colleen.

As a result of this I was able to go back to work. However, there was one problem, another year and a half of treatment and hospital stays.

My husband ended up taking on the day-to-day care for Colleen as he eventually had to give in to the stress and his work suggested he take some time for himself. After his leave he was laid off from a shortage of work. He has just now re-entered the workforce after trying to work part-time driving a school bus in between hospital visits.

I'll never forget the feeling I had when I was talking to the nurse when she first called. I had to come completely unglued in order for her to realize I was suffering. It's not a nice feeling to lose control of yourself; you only hope you can have enough strength to pull yourself back together.

There is no darker place to be than in a tortured mind. I guess it's hard for people to know how much you are suffering if you try to keep a stiff upper lip and wear a thin smile. Mental stress is not that easy to measure because you can't see it.

As I write this book I am sitting on my couch with my foot up on a pillow. I had some foot surgery and I am wearing a cast and using crutches. I had no trouble at all having my short-term income protection approved by my insurance company. You can see the cast, and you rely on a surgeon's advice for recuperation. How come it has to be this way?

I am grateful for my employer's benefits and am happy to be working. I just don't understand how anyone in the position of making decisions on whether or not someone's leave should be approved, can think that parents aren't damaged mentally when their child becomes gravely ill?

Unfortunately, compassion is something that is freely offered, and seldom felt. Several parents I have talked to have similar stories. What is wrong with this picture? And where is our government when its citizens need help?

Maintenance Treatment

Things started to become routine after Colleen's initial chemo regimen slowed down. At first, we were in-patient for the most part of the summer and, when we weren't, we were going in three days a week.

By September it had slowed down to once a week intermingled with five-day, pre-planned, in-patient stays. Thrown in unfortunately were unplanned admittances due to fever and neutropenia where she needed to be hooked up to an IV and blasted with antibiotics and antifungals and antivirals.

Colleen started school with her in-home teacher, Mary McClory, a retired school principal from her school. She was also teaching the other little girl from Colleen's school who was getting treated for leukemia. Both girls were too sick to go to school, and had too many hospital stays ahead. Their diagnoses were only a couple of months apart.

These hospital stays were such a nuisance because they had nothing to do with her cancer treatments, but more with the side effects of treatment. Often, she would miss out on a chemo treatment and because we were on a strict schedule, never got to go back and load up on missed medicine.

It was always a concern for most parents and doctors for a child to be delayed or miss out because the cancer was so unpredictable and the children needed all they could get to fight the beast hiding in their bodies.

DECEMBER, 2003

"Good afternoon, thank you for calling Scotia Bank, Sharon speaking, can I help you?" I said into the phone in my office just as my last client was leaving after having signed their mortgage documents.

It was December 21 and my last day of work for the Holidays. I had been back at work since the beginning of October and Danny was taking up the vigil with Colleen. She was currently an in-patient at CHEO in an isolation room and had been there for about a week and a half.

Earlier in December

It was a very strange Holiday season that year. Colleen seemed to have some sort of mission in mind as the calendar turned from November to December. She kept talking of Christmas and Santa and how she really wanted to be home for the Holiday.

Usually I leave visiting Santa until nearer the 25th, but this year she insisted on going the first of the month. I still have her picture with her brother from that year and you can see how sick she was, and a glimpse of what was to come.

She also was to have her first communion that year but for some unknown reason, we had arranged for it to happen in early December instead of May with her classmates. We knew she would not be in school, so when the suggestion was made, we jumped on it.

Her home school teacher helped her prepare for the big day and I managed to find some lovely communion clothes. She only had a few strands of blond hair hanging from her head, but she put a braid in them, and we tied a ribbon around her forehead. She looked like an angel as she entered the church to receive the Body of Christ.

The priest was there, and a few teachers, my other children, and my sister Pam and her husband were also there. It was a beautiful private ceremony as Colleen was currently running a fever and we knew that she was likely neutropenic and highly susceptible to infection so couldn't be around many people. We knew it wouldn't be long before the thermometer hit 38.5 and we had to go to the hospital and be admitted, but we were praying that she would be able to have her communion first.

It seemed very important to Danny and I and Colleen that she do this, and as the month went on, we knew why we all felt the foreboding and impending events that followed.

The next day was a hospital day after the communion. I had managed to get the day off to take her into CHEO. I had told my boss that I was worried and would not be able to concentrate unless I took care of making sure she was going to be OK. Fortunately I had some personal obligation days left and was able to do this with pay.

Her temperature was now at the point where we would have to go in but we were already headed there. I was really worried about her as she did not look or sound right. She was more tired than usual. Her colour was completely white. She was having difficulty breathing and was not at all interested in any food.

This was not normal for her even considering all her treatments. She loved to eat. Since last night things seemed to have got progressively worse.

"Colleen, get your coat, Honey, it's time to go to the hospital," I said as I gathered the remainder of her medicine that I would need to give her during the day.

When the children were not admitted to the hospital and only came in for day treatments, it was the parent's responsibility to keep track of all the chemo and other pills the children needed to take. The prescriptions were phoned into your local drugstore and you had to pick them up there.

You then had to consult your "road map" which forms part of your "protocol" and know the day, the time, the amount, and the frequencies of the dosages of up to seven or eight pills at a time.

There were chemo pills, and several pills to offset the side effects of chemo and it was quite a job keeping it all straight. The next task was getting the children to take the pills, and then sometimes, fishing through vomit to see which pill was thrown up and had to be re-administered.

I particularly liked my husband's approach to giving the medicine. He would put all the pills on a plate and then serve her the plate with a big glass of water. He pretended he was like a waiter and would wait around for the empty plate when she was done.

"Mommy, I don't want to go to the hospital today." Colleen said as if sensing some unforeseen delays in coming home for Christmas.

"You know we have to go, Baby, and your temperature is going up too. We may have to be admitted so I'm bringing some stuffed animals for your room just in case and some PJ's," I said as I was also pulling the Barbie comforter off her bed.

"Will I be home for Christmas?" She asked sounding rather distressed.

"I hope so Colleen, it's still over two weeks away" I said silently crossing my fingers behind my back "And if for some reason we can't come home, Santa will know where you are."

"No!" She cried now, "I want to be home!" She said with defiance and I thought to myself how in the world I would be able to maintain her spirits if she had to be in the hospital for Christmas.

Her upbeat spirit and outlook was 50 per cent of the reason she was overcoming so many obstacles and doing so well with the chemo. As long as we had something to look forward to, she could give it that extra effort and swallow the pill, or whatever else she needed to do, in order to arrive at our future plans.

The strategy was working so far, so I didn't want to concentrate too much on her not being home as she wanted. The other nagging thing was that when she had gone to see Santa with her brother a few days ago, she told Santa that the only thing she wanted for Christmas this year was to be at home with her family.

You've never seen a mall store Santa start crying so quickly in your life. He looked at me, and I shrugged, and then he went on to say that he will do the best that he could.

As expected, we were admitted on the spot once her blood tests confirmed low counts and her fever started to reach 39.5 degrees. We settled into her room and waited to be hooked up.

I called my husband and told him I was going to stay the night and that I had brought clothes for work the next day. Could he please be here by 11:00 a.m. so I could be at work by noon?

"Is she OK?" He asked after he had got the phone back from the other children I had just said goodnight to.

"I don't think so, Dan. She doesn't look right. She's very tired and sick. Her tongue is completely covered in fungus and while she's still managing to eat now, it could get a lot worse," I said remembering the mention of feeding tubes if it became necessary when speaking with the doctors earlier. "They have really strong antibiotics going into her because they suspect a serious infection somewhere. She's also got cold sores that are not healing so they have a really strong antiviral."

"Does she need me to bring anything tomorrow?" He asked feebly feeling powerless to help his little girl. "I can bring in something that she likes to eat."

"Good idea. Pick up some YOP. She needs the yogurt to counteract the antibiotics because I think she's also getting a yeast infection. She says it's painful to go to the bathroom." I wondered if there would be a nurse handy to help him put on antifungal crème if it became necessary.

I knew it would be a few days before the weekend and I would be back to take my shift when the work week ended, but I was concerned she would need to have a vaginal topical application to help relieve some of her pain and I knew it would make her Daddy uncomfortable.

For the next while I went to work, came home, looked after my other babies, and tried to focus on the positive. Time was slowly ticking closer to December 25th, and Colleen wasn't getting any better.

Danny was still with her and I would come for one overnight during the week to relieve him. We had switched places from the summer months. Each time I talked to her she wanted to know when she could come home. I didn't have words to say. I started pressuring the doctors and asking for exceptions.

"It's all she wants for Christmas," I pleaded with her oncologist one day, "Just to be home with her family"

"Sharon, we want that too, but she's too sick. We can't let her go. Why don't we just wait and see what happens, there's still some time" said Dr. Mandell with a look on her face that said don't count on it. Dr. Klassen was not looking after Colleen on this admission.

Around December 20th it became obvious that she wasn't coming home for Christmas.

Danny had called me at work and he was very upset from a very rough night. She had almost bled to death in his arms. Her platelets were so low that she was not clotting in her blood.

No matter how many platelets they got into her they didn't stick. She was blowing her nose a lot and having trouble breathing. They had just decided to put her on oxygen and she wasn't eating or drinking anymore.

They were bringing in the feeding tubes today so she could have nourishment.

"Her nose started to bleed and we couldn't stop it," he said as if still in shock from what happened. "The nurse was scared too. There were buckets and buckets of blood."

"Oh, my God! How is she now?" I demanded. Why wasn't I there? Guilt was flooding over me in great waves.

"She's fine now. We got it to stop finally, but she was also panicking," he said now starting to sound calmer.

"Danny, do you need me to come now or do you have everything under control?" I asked mentally thinking it was only another day before I would be off for two weeks and could be with her full-time.

At that moment I just wanted to walk right out of the bank and go to her no matter what the consequences. But I had to trust him, and I had to think of the other children too.

"No, Sharon, it's OK, she's fine now, and I can do one more night. You finish your work," he said trying to persuade me not to panic and that all was fine.

Of course I soon learned he was not telling the truth. I don't know if he actually realized at that moment how close we were to losing our little girl. It's not something the doctors normally come out and say I guess, especially when it could go either way.

"All right, I'll take your word for it, but I want to talk to her." He connected me up with her in her room.

"Hi, Baby, how are you feeling?" I asked trying to sound cheerful.

"Fine" was a reply so weak that I needed to strain to hear her words.

"I'll see you soon, OK?" I said as Danny took the phone and told me she was speaking through her oxygen mask.

"She sounds so weak from a few days ago, Danny. How does she seem about Christmas?"

"She seems to have accepted it for now. There's a lot of people coming through the hospital and dropping off presents and Teddy Bears to the kids. She had one of the Ottawa Senators give her a hat," he said trying to make it sound as if all was fun and festive in isolation on the cancer ward.

"OK then. My sister Col and Laura and Dave are coming for Christmas Eve to be with the other kids. We need to discuss which one of us will be at home and who will be at the hospital", I said trying to make an effort at some plans so as not to spoil Ella and Ryan's Christmas.

We haven't told them much and they have no idea their sister is fighting for her life. "You usually like to be home on Christmas Day, so you do Christmas Eve there and I'll come in and relieve you for the morning." I said making it sound all very sensible.

"Maybe the hospital will allow her some visitors considering the SARS scare has settled down a bit." So we ended the call and I made a mental note to call the hospital and ask the next morning.

December 21, 2003

"Hello Sharon, it's Dr. Chris from the hospital returning your call. What can I do for you?" She asked. I could hear all the familiar hospital sounds behind her.

"I was wondering if Colleen could have some visitors for Christmas Eve for awhile." I said sounding hopeful.

"Sharon, aren't you at all worried about what's going on with Colleen?" She asked in an oddly curious tone.

"What do you mean?" I replied now starting to get terrified. What didn't I know and what was I missing? I still had half the day before I could get there and be finished work.

"She doesn't look good, Sharon, we're worried about her," she said trying to sound less worried than what I was starting to hear in her voice.

And here I was trying to plan a party in her room! What kind of mother was I? I knew there was something terribly wrong yesterday, but I had let Danny calm me down so I could keep up things on the home front and keep things together.

It was too late now; nothing was keeping me another second.

"What's happening?"

"She's usually got so much spirit, but it's gone. She's just lying there."

"Thanks for telling me this doctor, I'm leaving now and will be there shortly." I said into the phone and hung up completely disregarding my earlier request.

"I have to go now, Ed. There's something wrong. The hospital told me they are worried about her." I was now panicking as I relayed my conversation with my boss.

"I agree you go now. But here," he said pulling a large parcel from behind his desk, "Your present. Open it now, you may need it"

I opened the large box and inside was a beautiful gift. It was an angel. Except this angel moved and held a light. It was beautiful and a tear came to my eye.

"Maybe it will brighten up your room, Sharon. Merry Christmas" he said with complete sincerity.

I sped home. I was trying to concentrate on what the doctor had said. I started to get the feeling I knew what was wrong. She needed energy. She needed my energy to fight. I would have to will it into her.

She was also very upset about not coming home for Christmas. She was giving up. I made up my mind right then and there that if she couldn't make it home for Christmas, then I was bringing Christmas to her!

OUR OWN VERY REAL CHRISTMAS MIRACLE

When I got to the hospital I could barely carry all the bags to the room. Before I had left home I went out to the stand of pine trees on our property and cut off some boughs. I was planning to use this as our Christmas tree and was hoping the smell of pine needles would overpower the familiar hospital aromas. I had also managed to put in a jar some of the homemade chicken soup I had made yesterday.

I was not prepared for the sight of my daughter when I entered her room.

Danny was sitting beside her bed with his head hanging low. He looked defeated like he had just lost an important battle. The room was dark and had an eerie quality to it. It was like the air stood still and the sounds were all muffled.

There was a nurse by the IV pole. Attached to it must have been 10 tubes. She was trying to determine which of the many hanging bags of liquid that the tubes were coming from was causing the IV pole to beep. I could sense her frustration at trying to unravel the puzzle.

There was someone lying in Colleen's bed. It was a little girl. All of her hair was gone and any hair that may have started to grow back was completely gone. She was on her back and was sunk so low in the covers on her bed that all you could see was her head and the oxygen mask completely covering her mouth. You could see her eyes too, that were currently closed.

As I moved closer to the bed her eyes opened and I knew it was her. The same deep blue eyes that up until now shone with a spirit so strong, now looking glazed and weak, let me know it was Colleen.

I gasped for breath and knew that I was almost too late. There was no energy in this room and everyone in it appeared to have already given up on my child. Even her father looked like he had resigned himself to the worst.

"Danny!" I said in a raised tone to stir him out of his deep thoughts. "Can you help me with these bags?"

He raised his head and I could see in his face he was exhausted and very relieved to see me. I think he had aged 10 years in the last few days since I had seen him.

"It's OK, I'm here now, I know what to do. Don't worry, she'll be fine. You get a rest." I said hoping the confidence was genuine I was trying to instill in my words. He kissed her goodbye, and hugged me tight.

"Call me later," he said and headed out of the room towards the elevators. God, this whole thing was horrible. He was too exhausted to talk and I didn't want to waste any time transferring my energy into Colleen and executing operation "Christmas Room". So I set about my preparations.

DECEMBER 23rd, 2003

I had seen him before. He was lingering outside baby Jordan's door when we were first admitted way back in May. I wasn't sleeping well at all then, and would get up and pace the halls.

At first he was startled when I caught a glimpse of him and he quickly disappeared. But I knew he was there. I could feel him watching. He was waiting patiently for his time.

Into early June baby Jordan's battle was coming to an end. What a strong little boy who had endured so much in his young life. His mother, a wonderful girl, had the gift of art.

She would always be in the playroom with Jordan and loved to help the other children with their crafts. We still have a pillowcase she helped Colleen draw on of some Disney characters.

The night before Jordan died I saw him again for just a moment. He was hiding; I saw a dark shadow in the hall across from the room.

The air was still so it was not hard to hear the muffled sobbing coming from inside the room. There was anguish in that room with no hope of any more anyone could do and death was waiting at the door.

My heart went cold when out of nowhere I saw a hand with a long bony finger emerge from a long flowing black cape and the finger was pointed at the room where Jordan was.

I panicked and started to run to warn the people inside, but I tripped, and couldn't get up, there was a big weight pushing me down, and I tried to scream to let them know….

I sat bolt upright in the cot sweat dripping from my brow. It was a nightmare. Except most of it was true. I don't remember seeing the angel of death outside Jordan's room, but I did feel the heaviness in the air and the immense grief of the occupants inside the room next to ours.

We had just started Colleen's chemo and everyone at the hospital filled our minds with hope that she would get better and survive. Yet right next door there was a baby boy dying from cancer. I wondered to myself if anyone else felt the mixed messages the way I did.

What strength the doctors and nurses must have to move from room to room, spread hope in one, and provide palliative support in another. I was relieved to hear that right next door to the hospital they were in the process of finishing off Roger's House, a pediatric palliative care facility, that would be finished in a couple of years.

In this place, families of children who were near death would have a homelike setting and afforded the dignity to be with their child and allowed to express their grief without the worry of upsetting another family who was at the beginning of their journey and had hope.

I think of how hard it must have been for Jordan's Mother, knowing he was so near death, to try to put on a smile for the other parents, whose children still had hope.

As the last vestiges of sleep cleared from my head I looked around the isolation room. I was very pleased with what I saw. After Danny left, I worked tirelessly hanging garland, slinging tinsel, and putting up Christmas lights in the room.

Colleen watched me as I carefully taped up the Christmas cards that were made for her by each child in her class at school. The last thing I did was turn on the moving angel and feel the glow of its light creep into the far corners of the room and brighten these dark places with life.

"Wow! What happened in here?" Said a stunned nurse who was just coming in on the day shift. "Are you sure I'm in the same room?"

"Mommy came and put all this up last night," said Colleen from her bed sitting up and pulling the oxygen mask away from her mouth so she could talk. "Today we're going to make a fireplace from the boxes over there and paint it so Santa will have a way to get in the room and leave me my presents."

"Isn't that going to be a bit small for Santa?" Said the nurse as a small smile was curving on the side of her mouth.

"No. Didn't you see the movie *The Santa Clause*? He's magic and can change shape too."

Feeling elated at the conversation Colleen was having with the nurse and sensing some of her spirit creeping back, I broke in, "Tell her what you had for supper last night, Colleen"

"What? You ate something?" Said an even more startled nurse.

"Well, I wouldn't go that far, but she did manage to get down five spoonfuls of the homemade soup I brought."

"It hurt," said Colleen, "but Mommy said that if I could get that down then I would start to get better."

"Yes, and we have another five spoonfuls for breakfast then lunch and by dinner we should be up to 10. Then I won't have any soup left, but I brought stuff to make some more," I winked at the nurse who was clearly thrilled at the overnight change in her little patient.

I was not going to let that angel of death anywhere near this room, and if he thought he might want to have a peek inside, then all he would see would be lights and decorations, and all he would hear would be laughter.

As the morning wore on it was obvious to me how weak Colleen had become. Where before I was able to form a routine to pass the time, now, there were too many interruptions and unexpected crises.

Her nose started to bleed again, but fortunately, it stopped sooner than it had the other night. She was coughing up bowls and bowls of mucus in attempts to breathe. She was weary from the strain and I sensed her losing the energy I had given her overnight.

She had already asked if she got better by tomorrow if she could go home, and I had to say no. I could see her deflate at the news and felt that I had in some way let her down. I had to think quickly about how to turn this around.

"Let's watch Home Alone. It will get us in the Christmas spirit and I have a little game we can play," I said determined not to give up.

I had found a box of musical instruments down the hall. There were Christmas bells and sleigh bells and tambourines and drums in the box. "I'll be right back, don't you go running off now," I said as I left the room praying that the instruments were still there and praying this plan would work.

"Now every time you hear music on the movie we have to shake these bells along with it. If you forget to shake, I get a point and vice versa." I said placing the sleigh bells in her hand that was lying limply beside her on the bed.

"Now move over a little, I'm going to snuggle up beside you so I'll be able to see if you're cheating or not." Colleen loves games and was highly competitive like everyone else in her family, and she took the bait.

At first it was like pulling teeth to get her to play. She was so tired and weak. I just had a feeling that the music and her playing would make her feel like she had some power to do something. Lying in bed with tubes and wires attached to every part of your body would definitely make me feel powerless.

I watched as she gently shook the bells. I joined along now too. The next time the music played on the movie, I shook first, and then she joined in. By the time we were halfway through the movie, not only were we shaking the bells louder, but singing along too.

Tears stung my eyes as I could see the life slowly slipping back into her body.

"Well, well, well, who do we have here?" Asked the visitor who unexpectedly came to the door. I couldn't believe my eyes. It was my brother-in-law, Malcolm, my deceased sister's husband.

He was carrying his guitar and was wearing his cowboy hat. He worked for the government around the corner and was on his lunch break to come in and play Christmas music for the kids at the hospital to cheer them up.

What a break! The movie had just ended and I was trying to

think of ways to keep her ringing those bells and singing. It was as if the music was bringing her back to life before my eyes.

"What a surprise, look Colleen, it's Uncle Malcolm," I said pointing to him in the door.

"Hi," she said raising the bells, "We were just playing."

I felt very special that Mal had come just when he did. It was another one of those moments when you know that someone is looking out for your child from above and was trying to say it's not her time.

Mal was led by angels and delivered to us to complete her healing and give her the strength to fight the illness overtaking her body. I wondered if my sister had anything to do with this. I could feel her presence in the room as soon as he walked in.

He got out his guitar and started to play. She wanted to sit up and at first it took her awhile to control her coughing while she cleared her lungs that had filled from her lying too low in the bed. When she was done, she picked up the bells and started playing along to his music.

I started to sing and shake the tambourine. Within minutes a nurse was in the room trying to see what all the noise was about. Then another came, then another, then in came some of the Child Life workers, and Molly Penny too.

We were all in the room and it was crowded with Christmas cheer, and people singing, and just for one moment I think everyone in that room forgot where they were and wallowed in the warmth of the season.

"I'll come back tomorrow, Colleen, if that's OK with you?" Said Mal as he was packing up his guitar. "It's Christmas Eve tomorrow and I wanted to stop by on my way home and play a few more Carols. You up to it you think?"

"Yeah!" Was her response.

Colleen got such a kick out of everyone in the room singing and collectively we had managed to lift her spirits so that now she was smiling. I guess she realized it wasn't going to be all that bad staying in here over Christmas, and now that she knew the nurses liked to sing, it made it all the better.

I knew I had to keep the momentum going, so I pulled out the boxes I had brought and we set about making the fireplace I had promised for Santa and we set up the boughs of the Pine trees to look like a Christmas tree.

We made paper decorations and she got out of bed to hang them on the tree. I had a plate from home that said "Santa's Cookies" and we placed it next to the freshly-painted fireplace. We then sat back, turned on the lights, and surveyed the room.

"Well, what do you think?" I asked her completely in awe of what had been accomplished in just over 24 hours.

The room was completely transformed, and with it, so was Colleen. When you came in the room from out in the hall it was like stepping into a whole new world. I felt life in the room and an idea came to mind that I hoped would continue to strengthen her spirit and resolve to get better.

"What do you think if we have a party for Christmas Eve? Auntie Colleen and Laura and Dave are coming tomorrow. We can make up some games like charades and pin the tail on the reindeer. I'll get the movie *The Christmas Carol*, and we can have that playing when they come"

I wish I had a camera to capture the look on her face when I made that suggestion. And then something else became very clear to me. She hadn't wanted to be left out of all the fun and games we usually play on Christmas Eve, and she figured since she was in the hospital, she would lose out. That would account for a large part of her low spirits and her reluctance to fight.

All I had to do now was clear it by the doctors and hope I didn't have to go back on my suggestion. Sometimes I have a tendency to put the cart before the horse, but I was really hoping that they would agree. It turned out they did and were so happy at the changes and improved health they encouraged it and played along for the fun.

CHRISTMAS EVE

I had managed to get more soup into her last night and I was starting to notice a difference in her energy level this morning. Last night I worked endlessly coaxing each mouthful past the fungus on her tongue and watching the brew slide down her throat.

A couple of the nurses just shook their heads in disbelief, but it was working. I had already held up this vigil before when I was trying to get the radioactive dye into her for the Gallium scan, and I was attacking this task with the same determination.

Malcolm came by first thing as promised and we had another little sing-song. This time a few doctors joined in taking a few moments from their rounds. There was widespread appreciation of the decorations and everyone congratulated Colleen on having the prettiest room in the hospital.

I watched as she grew stronger with each remark and actually started to feel uplifted myself.

By mid-afternoon we were busy finishing off the games and prizes for the party we had planned that night. I had packed a nice little dress for Colleen when she came in a couple of weeks ago. I must have had some premonition of what was to come, so my subconscious directed me without my fully understanding my motives.

It all felt like it was meant to happen as I slipped the hospital gown from over her head and put on her black velvet dress. I had managed to slip out for an hour as one of the Child Life Workers offered to stay with her while I went out and did a little Christmas shopping.

Danny and I didn't have much time considering the situation and I wanted to have something for Colleen and the other kids to open together and a few snacks for the party.

Around seven o'clock we were all ready. The lights were turned on, the movie was playing, the presents were wrapped and under our makeshift tree, and I put a fake flame in the hearth of our fireplace.

Colleen had managed to eat some jello and drink some water so everyone was feeling exhilarated at her progress.

"Mommy, do you think they will let me come home tomorrow?" She looked at me beseechingly. I could tell she knew the answer, but I could see her same spunk coming back. Usually she never gave up trying to get what she wanted. My little girl was back.

"You know the answer to that, Sweetie, but I'll tell you what. Daddy's staying overnight and I'll ask him to keep reminding the doctors that the only thing you wanted for Christmas was to be at home with your family. I know Daddy, if there's anyway at all possible, he'll find it. But don't go getting disappointed, OK?"

"OK," and I could tell she was fine with it if she couldn't make it home, but I also saw the stubborn set to her jaw and knew that she would be on her father's back to make it happen. But I knew it would be impossible.

Despite the fact she was improving and getting the best of her condition, she was still hooked up to at least eight bags of fluid and a morphine drip for pain. I'll always marvel at how she acted so normally and "with it" considering all of the medicine pouring into her veins.

They arrived and the party started. They brought more gifts and now you almost couldn't see the top of the makeshift tree.

We played our games and ate our snacks. We invited in some nurses to join in the fun and also opened the presents.

It was a miracle. Colleen seemed to draw on some inner strength that ran very deep as she went about twirling her brother to play pin the tail on the reindeer.

Eventually it was time to go. It was a bittersweet moment for me. It had been wonderful for us all to be together on Christmas Eve and we all made the most of it. But now I was going home and leaving Danny and Colleen behind. I tried to push the grief and pain away and remember the feelings of joy.

"Well, goodnight, Little Missy. You have to get to sleep so Santa can come. And Ella and Ryan need to get home to bed too. I'll be back tomorrow afternoon."

CHRISTMAS DAY

"Merry Christmas," I yawned as I entered the kitchen and saw my sister already busy at work cooking bacon. She was such a Godsend that year. There was no possible way Danny or I could keep up the Christmas traditions for our other two children, so she just stepped in and took over.

"How'd you sleep?" She asked, taking out some sausages from the fridge.

"Horrible, to tell you the truth. I miss Danny. I hate sleeping alone. I wonder if Santa made it to the hospital."

"Well, he sure made it here. Look at the presents he left for the kids. I heard them at four o'clock this morning snooping around. They're back to sleep now."

I had heard them too. I was happy that they were happy but I was so sad that Colleen wasn't here. They all had got what they had asked Santa for, except her.

It wasn't a good feeling for me knowing that she would be let down. It was out of mine and Santa's control though and there was nothing that could have been done differently. We made the best of it, and now I had to get over it and get on with it for the others.

We ate our big breakfast and then started to open the presents. I put a smile on my face and tried to look like I was having a terrific time. Unfortunately my mind was at the hospital. I was waiting for Danny to call because I knew how things were unpredictable there and you needed just the right window of time to call home.

The phone rang.

"Sharon? Merry Christmas!" It was Danny. He was sounding happy.

"Merry Christmas, Danny, how was the night?" I asked praying things went well and Colleen continued to get stronger.

"It was incredible. We saw the real Santa. He came into our room. He was dressed in old red robes and had a big white beard," he said sounding like a little kid again. "I mean it Sharon, it was amazing!"

"Are you sure you weren't seeing things?" I asked him, happy that they seemed to have such a good night.

"No. It was like the Polar Express Santa. Colleen was in awe. He was the real deal Sharon." He said trying to make sure I understood that he was thoroughly convinced.

"That's great, I'm glad. Maybe next year he'll come back and visit us at home. Hopefully we won't have to go through this again," I said praying silently that we never had to be in the hospital over Christmas again. "Before I talk to Colleen, what time do you want me to come?"

"We're coming home"

I thought I must be hearing things and for just a second there was silence on the phone.

"Stop kidding, you're being cruel" I shouted into the phone. Time stood still.

"No Sharon, it's true. Colleen's doing so well the doctors agreed to unhook her for a few hours so she could come home." Actually what happened is that Colleen nagged her father who nagged Dr. Mandell who finally gave in.

The room started to spin and I couldn't believe what I was hearing. This couldn't be possible. How?

"Are you serious?"

"Yup, they are just unhooking her now and giving her a three-hour pass"

It was 50 minutes each way, so that gave us about an hour at home. One hour, but at home. She got her wish!! I was crying as I relayed the message to everyone else in the room. I was never so grateful for anything, and I was so amazed at the flexibility and understanding of the hospital to satisfy a sick child's only Christmas wish.

I watched as Danny opened the door to the car and Colleen stuck out her feet to walk into the house. It was nothing short of a miracle. We were all crying at the marvel unfolding before us.

She had a determined look on her face and she stood very tall as she marched up to the front door. As she stepped over the threshold I could see accomplishment in her eyes. She was happy.

After all the hugs were given, she walked straight to the tree to check out all the presents her brother and sister had gotten. What a child! Was she more determined to come home to be with her family? Or was she bent on making sure her siblings didn't get more than her? She turned and faced us.

"I'm so happy." She said as her brother came over and joined her and they started to play a game that he had not yet opened.

It was a wonderful time and I struggle to find the words to describe a truly incredible, unexpected, and life-altering time. The hospital ended up calling just as we were getting ready to leave.

"Sharon, don't rush back. I was talking to the doctor, and you still have 2 hours before her next medications. Take another hour. I'll make sure everything's ready to go when you get back," Brenna said conspiratorially into the phone.

This day was getting better and better. I told everyone what was said and we settled back into relaxing and enjoying each others' company.

The turkey was now cooed and my sister had worked hard at trying to make sure the dinner was ready before we headed back. The extra hour would allow us to eat together.

"Dinner's ready! Time to eat."

When she had time to cook and stuff a turkey is still a mystery to me this day, not to mention the mashed potatoes, Brussels sprouts and other trimmings. I don't remember seeing her in the kitchen, but then again, my focus was elsewhere and it had been a very long time since we were all home together as a family under the same roof.

Colleen wasn't able to eat much because her tongue and mouth was still a problem, but she picked at her plate and moved the food around in an effort to fit in.

"This is good, Auntie Colleen," she managed and tried to swallow a mouthful of gravy.

It was time to go. We packed Colleen up in the car and I said my good-byes as I was headed back to the hospital now. It was hard leaving, but I felt so blessed that God had allowed us this time by directing the Angels to send my brother-in-law with the music, and that the doctors had granted us this reprieve.

Back in the room much later, I started to get hungry. Colleen was now sleeping and the end of *The Grinch Who Stole Christmas* was playing on the TV.

I snuck out of the room and went to a pay phone. I ordered a small pizza and had them deliver it to the hospital. I went back to the room with my snack and realized that it would be a turkey sandwich I would be munching on at home at this time of night. I didn't care though; this was the best Christmas ever.

The lights were still casting a soft glow over the room, and the tinsel twinkled brightly as it slowly rippled in the air circulating in the room. I will never forget that Christmas and the miracles that unfolded and know without a doubt that we almost lost our daughter but somehow with everyone's help and prayers, we brought her back.

NEW YEAR'S EVE

We got an overnight pass on December 31st six days later. Colleen had continued to gain strength and get better. We had a few more visitors like my sister Pam and her husband Dave, and Colleen's

Home-School Teacher, who brought well wishes and whose presence was like fuel to her spirit.

"Be back by 11:00 a.m. tomorrow" said the nurse to me as she was carefully unhooking Colleen. She was now down to only a couple of IV bags as the morphine and feeding tubes were gone.

"I'm just so thrilled that the doctors have given us this overnight pass. It's a 24-hour 'get out of jail free card' to me." I said with a hint of laughter in my voice.

"You're not the first parent to feel that way." She said finishing her task.

"I don't mean to sound ungrateful, but sometimes it seems like a prison and the doctors are the jailors. I know that they are just doing what's best for our children. I never dreamed that there were things like overnight passes and day passes, but I'm really glad there are." I said getting Colleen's coat.

"Yes, they are good. It helps the kids get away and into a different environment for awhile. You live close enough to go home so that's good. The families that live far away often get overnight passes to Ronald McDonald House where the family can all be together, it seems to help with everyone's coping."

The New Year rang in with us all banging Pots and Pans on our front porch. Fortunately there's a lot of space between our houses so I don't think we disturbed the neighbors.

We had a quiet night and played some games and had some snacks. We all watched the TV as the countdown to midnight came.

As I tucked the children into their beds I wondered what surprises the year 2004 would bring and I prayed silently that we would all still be together to ring in 2005.

THE YEAR 2004

Colleen was discharged shortly after New Year's day. I am pleased to say that we have not to this date had quite the same scare that we did that Christmas. We never take anything for granted anymore, and we know how precious our time is together, and how it can be taken away in any moment.

I am convinced that Colleen must have some bigger purpose in her life. Why else would her life have been spared? I know of countless other children who have not been so fortunate, who died from the exact complications she had. Why them and not her?

As the year waned on it seemed that news was constantly coming in that children were relapsing with their disease, or dying from it. The doctors always did their best with each patient, and tried so hard, but some children lost their battles and went on to become little angels in heaven.

March, 2004

"You're all set, here are the tickets. Have a great trip," said the representative from the Children's Wish Foundation. "I'm sure you'll have a terrific time being together as a family, you deserve it."

Just after New Year I realized that Colleen was doing a lot better, but I also knew we were headed into some harder chemo. It was also flu season and there were more bugs flying around in the hospital than anywhere else.

I discussed it with Danny and we both agreed Colleen needed something to look forward to, and our family needed a break. We had been given a card by a representative from the Children's Wish Foundation when we were initially being treated with the understanding that we could call anytime when Colleen was ready to make her wish.

"Colleen, Daddy and I were talking, and we were wondering if you wanted to make your wish now?"

She looked delighted that were having this conversation. A little friend of hers from the hospital who was being treated for leukemia had just come back from her wish trip to Disneyland and Colleen had been so excited thinking about the possibility of her going some day.

"Really, can I make my wish now?" She asked excitedly.

"Yes, Honey, we've talked to the doctors and they feel by March you should have most of the harder chemo done, and it would be a good time for you to go. Mommy managed to get the time off as well from work. What's your wish?"

She wasted no time in telling me that she wanted to go to Disneyland and I promptly picked up the phone and called the Wish Foundation. We were almost half way through her treatment, and I instinctively knew this was the right time to go for everyone.

A lot of families leave their wishes until the end of treatment, and some families don't make them at all. With the scare of Christmas still fresh in my mind, I was still not completely confident Colleen would make it to the end of treatment which was over a year away.

I was constantly trying to push out the memories of the deaths of my parents and sister to this disease, and I was afraid that the cancer would come back with a vengeance to attack her before her treatment was done.

The hospital seemed to agree too that it was a good idea and that it might be a good way to mark the half way and recharge everyone's batteries for the second half.

We had the most special time and I couldn't be thankful enough to the Wish Foundation for making it possible. We would never have been able to afford this vacation, especially now, considering all of our extra expenses and lost income.

The memories of all of my children and my husband at Disneyland as we went on rides and got our pictures beside Mickey Mouse and Donald Duck will forever be a memory from which I know I will find solace and happiness for the rest of my life.

What topped off the trip even more was that my sister Pam and her husband were in Florida at the same time as we were, and they "dropped by" to say 'Hi'. I know my sister carries the same memories with her of the magnificent gift given to our family by so many generous, caring people who support the Children's Wish Foundations.

Being brought back to Reality

Colleen's fever didn't spike until we were at the Airport on the way home from Disneyland. The day before I was afraid that her fever might get too high and that we would have to be airlifted from the Disney Cruise to the nearest hospital.

Sometimes this happens and it is terrible for the children to have to leave their Wish. Our plane was scheduled to leave in a couple of hours and there was really little else we could do but wait.

We had brought her chemo with us on the trip and she was due for a dose. I knew that by giving her the chemo it would drop her counts even more and the infection that she must be battling would have a better chance of making her worse.

Her kidneys had just recovered from the strong medicines she had received at Christmas to combat the fungus overtaking her mouth and I worried that we would have to go through that again and that she'd end up on dialysis.

She had to take up to 12 huge pills everyday for the entire

month of January that was equivalent to 200 bananas to replace the potassium and repair the holes in her kidneys from side effects of the medicines.

Fortunately she took the pills, and could swallow them, or it could have been a lot worse for her in the long run.

"It's Colleen's mom, Sharon, I'm calling from the Orlando Airport, and may I speak with the oncologist on call?" I asked the receptionist at CHEO in Ottawa.

"Sure, stay on the line and I'll get someone on the phone"

You never knew who you were going to get. Colleen was treated by a team of *o*ncologists and they all took their turns being "on call" 24 hours a day, seven days a week.

It was so comforting knowing you could pick up the phone from anywhere and speak to a doctor that knew your child well and would give you the proper guidance needed to make sure they would be all right. This kind of care is not something the general population is used to, and it is something that takes a while to get weaned from once your child's treatment is over.

You get so used to picking up the phone and calling an oncologist for help, that when your child is all better, and off treatment, it's difficult to accept that now you must go back to the way you were before the cancer and call the Family Doctor.

It took me awhile personally, but the hospital staff was patient, and I had good faith in my Family Doctor. I also think it took the Family Doctor awhile to get used to it too because she had not been part of Colleen's care for the last two years, and now she was entrusted with a child in remission from a very aggressive form of cancer, and it was her job to stay on top of every illness and rule out relapse.

"Give her the chemo and some Tylenol. If she's still febrile when you get back home, give us a call." And with that the Oncologist said goodbye.

As it turned out she still had a fever when we got home and, after calling the hospital again, they told us to come in. It turned out that she had an infection in her liver and so she got hooked up to very strong antibiotic that eventually made her better.

In retrospect I don't at all feel bad for Colleen having to be admitted to the hospital so soon after Disneyland. Everyone was asking her about the trip, and looking at the pictures. She was so happy and so energized, that it was no trouble for her at all overcoming this illness.

Perhaps this liver condition was what I sensed coming and the reason why it was so important to have her Wish. Could this have potentially been another replay of Christmas? In any case, we were discharged in five days and things went back to the regular routine of home and hospital.

By June she was still doing very well despite the odd complication here and there. Sometimes the chemo would make her very sick and she would throw up whatever she had eaten.

I'll never forget one Sunday night, sitting at the dining room table, having dinner with my family. I had worked hard all day making Roast Beef, roast potatoes and Yorkshire Pudding the way my mom had taught me years before. I had lit the candles and the music by John McDermott was playing softly from the CD player in the other room.

It was a very nice atmosphere and I was mentally taking a picture in my mind of everything and thinking how blessed we were to be sharing this moment.

We were halfway through dinner when Colleen threw up all over my new tablecloth and into the half finished bowl of salad. She had tried to stand up to make it to the bathroom, but she couldn't make it.

Ella, Danny, Ryan and I didn't know what to do at first because it happened so fast and was completely unexpected. She was looking at us, then down at her vomit on the table. I could see she was going to cry so I got up right away.

"No big deal, Honey" I said grabbing paper towels from the kitchen. "We'll just clean this up and get you a new plate." I had set the tone and the rest of the family followed along.

"Gross! Mom, I hope you don't expect me to eat any more salad now?" Said my son trying to do his part to make light of the situation.

"It's OK Col, I really didn't want any more salad either, thanks for making sure Mom didn't make us eat more before dessert," said Ella from her seat across the table.

Colleen smiled. My husband took her to get cleaned up while I cleared off the table cloth and put a new one on. Within minutes we were all back seated at the table as if nothing had happened.

The rest of the evening went well, and eventually Colleen's queasiness subsided with the help of Ondansetron, a very effective anti-nausea pill designed especially for chemo patients.

In early July

Colleen was asked to help start the first ever Hudson's Bay Marathon being held in Ottawa. Proceeds from the run were going to CHEO among other hospitals, I think. I was very proud of her as she stood in front of hundreds of people and proudly fired the gun to start the race.

Actually it was more like a tube filled with confetti, and I was holding it with her. It backfired into my stomach and I had a bruise from that for weeks. My bruise and my obvious mishandling of the device has been a source of constant teasing over the years.

The rest of the Summer

It was very relaxing and relatively undisturbed. We would get away to the trailer when we could and when she was well enough. She loved to fish and so we spent many hours out on the water as a family.

I would make a picnic lunch and we would pull up to an island. I'd spread out the blanket and lay down our buffet. I made sure to avoid the island where she had contracted the Prickly Parsley last year.

Sometimes we pulled up to an island with a fire pit. My husband would light a fire and clean the fish that we had just caught. I always came prepared with a fry pan and oil, so many a time we sat basking in the sun enjoying fresh fish filets.

Eventually Fall came

It was time to start getting ready to go back to school. She was still taking chemo and so was highly susceptible to infection. The home-school teacher we had last year was now officially retiring and was planning to travel. The hospital seemed to think it would be good for Colleen to attempt to go back to school and be with her peers.

I listened with apprehension and reluctantly agreed that we needed to try. Marilyn, our Interlink Nurse from the hospital met me at the school with the principal and her teacher to discuss re-integration.

"What about hygiene?" I asked Mr. Guertin, the principal. "Are there Purell bottles in all the classrooms so the kids don't spread their germs?"

"No, we don't have that. Some of the teachers bring them to the class for the kids, but it's not a routine" silently knowing that it would be almost impossible to get all the kids to use the hand sanitizers on a regular basis.

"OK, well I'll make sure she has some of her own." I said already thinking of the lecture I was going to give Colleen about using the sanitizer religiously.

"Sharon, do you have any other concerns?" Marilyn asked me. "This is the time to express your fears and make a plan with the school."

"Nope, it's just "wait and see" what happens I guess. She's still going to the hospital once a week now though; she's going to miss a lot of school. You won't be calling any truancy officers on us will you Mr. Guertin?" I joked as I could sense the meeting was over and now we just had to move forward and see what happened.

At the end of the school year it turned out she was only absent from class 65 days due to illness and hospital appointments. My husband and I worked hard with her at home on her school work and she managed to pull off all A's and B's in Grade 3.

In mid September

It was time for the annual Terry Fox Run. Colleen was named "Terry Fox's Official Team Member" and helped kick off the run in our local community. She couldn't walk the entire 10 kms as she was still weak from taking her daily chemo, but we managed to borrow an adult stroller from the local Community Living for the day and so when she needed a break she could sit and be wheeled around.

She was such an inspiration and I believe a lot of money was raised that day for cancer research.

A setback

A couple of months later I was making a plan to rent two wheelchairs from our local Drug store.

Some side effects of chemo are brittle bones. She had been playing on a play structure with some friends and jumped down about two feet to the ground.

When she had asked me if she could go play with her friends I was hesitant at first because I sensed something could happen. I had quickly dismissed my worry and told her to go and play but to be careful.

Within minutes one of the children whom she was playing with at the arena where my son was playing hockey rushed over to me and told me Colleen was hurt. I ran as fast as I could to find her lying on the ground.

At first I thought she was kidding about the pain because I saw how far she had jumped and it was hardly any distance to break a bone.

"Come on Colleen, get up, and try to walk on it - it will feel better" I said trying to help her up.

"It hurts too much, Mommy," she said between tears. "I can't walk."

After a few seconds I started to realize this was more serious than I thought. I asked someone to get my husband. Danny and I lifted Colleen into the car and arranged for someone to bring Ryan home after his game.

The hospital confirmed that she had a broken ankle in a couple of places. For two weeks and until the swelling went down she was not allowed a cast. She could not put weight on her foot. She would need a cast for six more weeks after that.

We had just got into the routine of going to school and reconnecting with all her friends and she loved it. I knew she would be devastated if she was pulled out now.

"I can't do it!" She shouted as she almost fell to the ground.

When we came home from the hospital with the crutches it became very obvious that she would not be able to maneuver on them. She didn't have the strength in her arms to support her weight and keep her foot off the ground.

She was also very discouraged she didn't have a cast so her friends had something to sign. I knew that this was another one of those moments that I would have to put my thinking cap on and come up with a solution so that she could go back to school, get around without putting weight on her foot, and have a cast to sign.

Her progress and health so far was directly linked to her positive attitude and outlook. I was worried that this fracture might set her back spiritually as well as physically and that some other more threatening concern would have its chance to overtake her. They had found my mom's lung cancer not long after she had fallen off a ladder and broken her arm.

I ended up taking the week off work to help her adjust. My boss was again very good and I had some unused vacation time I was saving for a moment just like this. Danny was working part-time but I felt this was again one of those moments that I would need to step in full-time and rebuild her world.

The first thing we did was move out most of the furniture so she could get around well on our ground floor in the house in a wheelchair. She had full access to her room and the bathroom and kitchen and fridge if she wanted. It was a good thing we live in a bungalow.

Then next I devised a plan and then we practiced several dry runs throughout the week. I would wheel her onto the front porch. She would put on the brakes while I went to get the truck. I would then drive up to the front porch across the grass.

I taught her how to slide down out of the wheelchair, onto her bum then down the stairs keeping her foot up in the air the whole time. I then showed her how to slide backwards into the car and get settled. I would then load the wheelchair into the trunk.

We practiced getting in and out of the car at different places. We went to Wal-Mart and the grocery store with her in the chair. She started to realize that despite her injury, with a few modifications, she would still be able to be part of everything the family was doing.

I was very grateful at this time for all of the hard work done by so many people who lobbied the government to have wheelchair accessible ramps and restrooms and make it so much easier for people with disabilities to get around and have freedom and dignity.

It's not until you are forced into a situation that you realize how important some things are and you can truly appreciate the efforts of so many who have had to endure without these luxuries but who can now know their efforts are appreciated.

Now we had to plan our routine around the school.

By Monday Colleen was very good at getting in and out of the house and truck. She was adept at the wheelchair and seemed very comfortable with her situation.

Every morning for the next eight weeks I would load Colleen into the truck and head for the school. I would park close to the front door. I had rented another wheelchair for the school and had it stored in the office.

I parked the car near the front door and asked her to wait while I got the wheelchair from the office. I would wheel it over to the truck and she would slide into it and then I wheeled her into the school and to her class.

At the end of the day my husband would go into the school, collapse the wheelchair in the office where Colleen was waiting, and then carry her onto his bus. After his run he would bring her home as he parked the bus in our driveway.

The first day I brought her, the entire class was eager to help her out and I could see she was in good hands.

"The kids are actually arguing over who will help her next," said Colleen's teacher, Mrs. Chapleau. She was an excellent teacher and we were blessed to have her.

As for the cast, I made a stocking out of some old material I had lying around. I glued green felt shamrocks and designs on it and cut out her name and sewed it on.

This was a big deal for me because when I had wanted to learn to sew from my mother years ago, and I was actually going to take the time to learn, the brain tumor she got from the cancer that had spread from her lungs, rendered her paralyzed and incapable of using her hands or walking and put her in a wheelchair as well.

I guess I managed to pick up a few of the basics though somehow, and successfully sewed a makeshift cast to cover her foot which lifted her spirits considerably and allowed her friends to sign their names with markers.

By Halloween

Finally Colleen had a real cast. It was covered with signatures from her friends. I still have the Angel costume she chose that year and I remember pushing her door to door as the wings kept getting in the way.

Christmas, 2004

Christmas was coming and it was only a couple of weeks away. Despite last year's Miracle, I still felt apprehension at the approaching date as the memories flooded back. It had been too close for comfort.

Colleen's cast was just off and we wanted to start making plans for the Holiday. She seemed to be coming down with something and everyone else in the family was also battling some bug. The good news was that she wanted to ask Santa for a Game Boy instead of being home with the Family. I took this as a good sign.

I was terrified that this would turn into the same nightmare as last Christmas and found it difficult to commit to anything knowing how things could change in an instant.

"Mom, we really want to come to Oakville and be with everyone. I know we were supposed to come last year, but there was no way with her being in the hospital," I explained to my Mother-in-Law long distance on the phone one day. "I don't want her to get sick and then for us to be stuck so far away in Sick Kids. I have to work on the 27th."

"I understand, Sharon; we will miss you all and hope to see you soon." I could hear the disappointment in her voice.

She was a lovely woman and a terrific mother-in-law. She was like a second mother to me and it was very important to have this connection considering I had lost my own mom when I was 25. Ella was only three months old when my mom lost her battle to cancer, and my mother-in-law has always been there as best she could.

"We'll try for Easter," I said hanging up the phone.

We decided to go to my sister's in Montreal. It was only two hours away from CHEO and if we needed to, we could get there faster than from Toronto. My sister outdid herself again and went out of her way like last year to make sure the family had a wonderful Christmas.

Unfortunately on Christmas Eve

We went to the Nutcracker at the Place Des Arts in Montreal. It was a gift for my family from my niece, Laura. While there, Colleen spiked a fever. It was a very good performance considering the fact that I was a little distracted.

We went straight to the Montreal Hospital to have her blood tested to see how strong her counts were and to determine if we needed to be admitted and hooked up for IV antibiotics.

Fortunately, she was just above the magic number and we were able to go back to my sister's. We spent Christmas Day and went home on Boxing Day.

"Please Father, is there any thing you can do? My wife needs help." My husband pleaded to the Priest in our local Church.

I was a mess ever since we had come home from the hospital in Montreal. I should have been happy that our Christmas did not turn out like last year, but I couldn't help myself and stop myself from feeling such despair. I was coming unglued emotionally and couldn't stop crying and the anxiety and panic attacks were in full swing.

I knew I had to go back to work the next day, and I knew I had to do something to pull myself together. I didn't want to take any more pills as I knew they would make me groggy the next day at work.

Danny had taken me for a drive to try to calm me down while my sister watched the children. He decided at the last minute to pull into the church.

The priest talked to me and I felt very comforted. This was the same priest who had given her a special blessing last December when she was so ill and told us to look for a miracle and that Colleen would get better by Christmas Eve. This blessing was made sometime between her communion and Christmas, I can't remember the exact date.

I thought back to when he said this and the confidence with which he spoke. Not that we didn't have faith, it's just that he was so sure of his words, and she was so sick, it was hard to imagine.

It all worked the way he said it would. That explained the angels directing my brother-in-law with the music that brought her back to life. So I silently said a prayer to God and asked him to give me the strength I needed to get over this and get control, so I would continue to be able to look after my family. I knew that if I fell apart, then everyone else would too.

I could lean on Danny as a rock most of the time, but the bad memories of last Christmas and almost losing Colleen came crashing back so fast that I needed more than just his strong arms and reassurances to keep me going.

By the time I left the church I was slowly putting a lid on my fears. The next morning I got up and went to work and it would be awhile before I was again brought to the brink of a complete nervous breakdown.

New Year's Eve, 2005

We rung it in again with the same pots and pans as last year, and we all gathered around the TV to watch the countdown at Times Square.

As I tucked the children in their beds I marveled that an entire year had gone by and by this time next year, God willing, we would again pull out the pots and pans and ring in 2006.

I could sense some challenges ahead and wondered what was in store as the days and months ticked by until the end of treatment.

The Year 2005

Colleen's health didn't get any better in January.

It seemed she was always sick. There were countless times we would drive into CHEO at 2 a.m. after having taken her temperature that was nearing 40.5 degrees, only to be sent home a few hours later.

This was new territory for us and it took a while to adjust to the new routine. Her chemo was getting less intense so her blood counts weren't affected as much. We still needed to call the hospital when her temperature hit 38.5, and we were still instructed to come in for a blood test to check her counts.

But for some reason her white blood cells and neutrophyl counts were in an acceptable level that didn't require hospitalization and a hook up to IV antibiotics. Even with this knowledge it didn't make sense why she kept getting so sick? We didn't complain though and were glad to make the trip back home instead of having to stay in for a week.

"I'll call down to the ER and let them know you're coming so you can go into an isolation room right away," said the Oncologist I had just contacted because her fever hit 38.9 as I was putting her to bed. "They'll do a blood test and we'll go from there."

"Thanks, Dr. Mandell," I said thinking that this was another of those special privileges we enjoyed.

I always felt a little pang of guilt when we got to the hospital and bypassed all the other children in the waiting room who had been there for hours, and got ushered to our own private room.

The only thing that made me feel OK about it was the knowledge that I would gladly switch with anyone of those parents in a second. I would rather wait for three hours in a waiting room at 2 a.m. than have a child with cancer any day.

In between Colleen's bouts of poor health we managed to do some nice family outings that year.

Max Keeping had invited our Family into his own private box at the Corel Centre to watch the Ottawa Senators playing a Hockey game. We were joined by a couple of other families whose children were well enough to go and we felt very special.

Max himself is a cancer survivor and he was so good with the kids. In his box it was all you could eat and all you could drink. I think my son must have consumed at least 10 cokes and 20 chicken fingers along with two pizzas and 12 egg rolls!

We were given tickets to a Musical production at the National Arts Centre as well as tickets to some other events at the Corel Centre, including tickets to see Hillary Duff in concert.

Wade Redden, who is one of the Ottawa Senators, has a box at the Corel Centre, and he often kept it open for the kids from CHEO to enjoy for selected events.

We were in a new reality. Colleen would be too sick to go to school, but would be too well to be admitted to the hospital.

It was hard to figure out how to keep both Danny and I working during this unpredictable time. Fortunately we had some backup that we could call on, like good friends of ours, whose child was home schooled.

Rebecca is a good friend to Colleen this day, and her mom didn't work outside the home at this time. When we were really stuck, Pam would let me drop Colleen off in the morning before I went to work. Danny would then go and get Colleen after his morning bus run. Then he would drop her off there for his afternoon run, and pick her up on his way home.

When Colleen was too sick to leave the house and we knew it wouldn't be fair to entrust her with Pam, we managed a different way. I would be late for work in the morning and would drive her to the school.

My husband would be finished his morning run at the school, and I would walk her over to his bus past all her classmates and load her onto his bus. He would then bring her home for the day and take care of her.

I would not take my lunch break until 3:00 o'clock in the afternoon and I would come home for an hour or so and look out for her until he came home awhile later. I would then go back to work for a few hours to make up my lost time.

Some days, it would be impossible for me to get away in the afternoon, so my oldest daughter Ella would take the day off school to look after her sister. I knew that this wasn't the best solution, but we had no other options.

Ella ended up coming home with a note one day from the school that said she had been absent too much, and was at risk of not graduating that year because she didn't have the board of education's required classroom time.

Ella was and still is a good student, and fortunately suffered no decline in marks for her part in taking care of her sister. My son wanted to be able to help too, but he was too young to properly take care of Colleen during her many nosebleeds and unforeseen health concerns.

As February slid into March

It became obvious that Colleen was spending more time at home than at school. She picked up a nasty virus and would spend all day on the couch coughing and blowing her nose. Danny and I were convinced there was something more sinister brewing deep within her body as there seemed to be no other reason she kept getting so sick.

Eventually she got pink eye in one eye. Her left eye was swollen shut and it was all we could do to keep the polysporin antibiotics flowing that would help clear up some of the pus and help her see.

Only when the pink eye spread to the other eye and now both eyes were swollen shut and blood red did the hospital decide to look for other causes. I guess it was that "wait and see" approach again.

"Sharon, we did a different blood test and it looks like Colleen is very low in one type of blood count" Deanna her nurse case manager told me as I was at my wits' end by now. "This is the reason she keeps getting so sick"

"What is it?" I asked, feeling relieved that they had found something and praying they could give her something to get her over all this illness that was so wearing on her and the entire family.

"We're going to start giving her some Immunoglobulin blood transfusions. There are antibodies in your blood that can sometimes be wiped out from the chemo. Her body is tired of the chemo now, and the constant illnesses tell us that she needs a little extra help to fight off the infections."

"OK, do it, anything to help her eyes," I replied from the phone in my office at work. I wondered why it took them so long to arrive at this conclusion, but then realized that Colleen's treatment followed a "wait and see what happens to her approach" and now enough time and misery had gone by before treating her.

The blood transfusions or IGG's were a compilation of several people's blood where they siphoned off the antibodies she needed, and converted them to liquid form to be transfused.

It is a costly formula reserved only for dire circumstances and when the patient was at risk of not getting any better. Colleen endured these transfusions well into 2006, a year later, as they routinely checked the levels of her blood and waited until her own body was producing these antibodies again.

By April she was better.

The Immunoglobulins were working. I called it her synthetic immune system. Usually just before we went to the hospital to get gassed up with another transfusion she would start to come down with something.

After she received the treatment, she would get better. It was like she literally ran out of gas and, once transfused, would be good for a few more weeks. She was also taking antibiotics every weekend on top of these transfusions, so she had lots of help to stay healthy.

May, 2005

"We're going to do one last lumbar puncture on Colleen before her end of treatment," the oncologist told us at the beginning of the month. "We want to be sure that there are no more cancer cells lurking in her spinal fluid."

"That would give us peace of mind, thanks." I replied to Dr. Klaus. May 24th would be her last day. We had come through the last two years with chemo everyday and soon it would be all finished.

Many parents approach this milestone with mixed emotions. Up until that day, we had established a routine around medications and were so busy following our protocol that we didn't think about when it would be all over.

Danny and I were apprehensive of this day because we knew the chemo she was getting was killing the cancer cells. What would happen when we stopped the chemo? Would the cancer come back?

"Good afternoon, Scotia Bank, Sharon speaking, can I help you?"

"Sharon?"

"What is it Danny? What's wrong?" I had been feeling apprehensive all day for reasons I couldn't explain. I had wanted to take Colleen to the hospital for her last Lumbar Puncture, but something came up at work and I couldn't get away. I rationalized my absence by remembering that the Lumbar Punctures she'd had in the past were more routine, and both of us didn't need to be there. She'd be back at home soon and it would be all over.

"They almost couldn't revive her. It was like her heart stopped and she wasn't breathing!" He said into the phone.

"What happened?" Here we go again. Poor Danny, was it his fate to be there every time she was in a near-death experience? Was it my fate to be here at work?

I was suddenly very angry at the fact that I had to work while she was so close to dying. I quickly set my thinking straight and lost the guilt. At least her father was with her.

"Her heart rate dropped to almost nothing from the anesthetics. They think the chemo has weakened her heart. Also, she's carrying around a lot of weight now from the steroids she's been on, when she was rolled on her side, she stopped breathing."

"Oh no!" I shouted a little too loudly and could tell I had

disturbed the clients in the next office. One of my colleagues walked by my door to make sure I was all right. I nodded that I was fine and went on asking questions.

"How did you revive her?"

"It was close, Sharon. The nurse with us was even crying and shouting for her to wake up. They did all sorts of things to try to get her to wake up and start breathing again."

"How is she now?" I asked knowing that she must be awake and fine or else Danny would be telling me some different story.

"She doesn't remember any of it. She's fine. She's playing with Molly Penny in the playroom."

It never ceases to amaze me, the resilience of children. She was near death one moment, playing the next.

"Are you coming home soon?" I asked hoping he would say they were on their way soon. I would have to make sure I got home in good time to be there when they came in and already have supper cooking so we could sit down to a family dinner.

"I'm just waiting for her counts, and then we'll be on our way."

May 24, 2005

After the lumbar puncture scare the rest of the month was taxing emotionally. I thought back on all the hurdles she had overcome and wondered if there were any more surprises that might pop up before the end of the month. As it turned out, all we did was needless worrying.

I was waiting for the marching bands and the trumpets to

sound announcing that this was Colleen's last day of chemo, but the day came and went with very little ceremony.

Danny and I weren't sure that stopping the chemo wouldn't bring with it more challenges and relapses so we didn't want to do too much. Colleen seemed a little strange too, because she knew it was all over.

She had made it! How much significance do you verbally attach to this moment that you have both dreamed of and dreaded for two years?

Some families bake cakes and bring them to the hospital. They light candles and share the cake with the other kids who are still undergoing treatment. My friend Kelly and her daughter Ashley had long ago finished chemo, and I remembered a conversation I'd had with her over a year and a half ago. I am happy to say Ashley is in remission and I think Kelly can now use the word "cured"!

"Go figure. Here I was so concerned about keeping Ashley away from the Chicken Pox, and one of the volunteers called the hospital the day after Ashley's party and said she had Chicken Pox!"

"Didn't she know she was sick?" I asked shaking my head at the irony of the whole thing. Chicken Pox is a virus that is deadly to children on chemo. They have a special drug we nickname 'Zig' that must be given as soon as you know your child has come into contact with someone who has Chicken Pox. I don't recall all the reasons, but just know that the hospital considers it a very serious thing, so we don't question.

"She says she didn't know. There were about 10 kids in the playroom and they've all had to have 'Zig' as a precaution." Poor Kelly, she was always so careful, too careful. I guess it just goes to show that no matter how hard you try to protect your children there's always something unpredictable that can come up.

I realized this a long time ago and maybe that's why I sometimes took calculated risks with Colleen by allowing her to go to a movie or play with a friend as long as she wore a mask and always washed her hands. So many things could go wrong, it wasn't fair to not let her live and enjoy what life she was able to have.

I know of many families that shelter their children so much and limit their activities that it becomes like a punishment to them that they have cancer. I have seen siblings of the children with cancer suffer too because they were not allowed to bring home friends and were denied sports and activities because of the financial burden of the illness.

Even though we couldn't afford it, we still kept our son in Hockey, and her sister went on a trip to Italy with her class. Fortunately my daughter baby-sat a lot and was able to finance most of this trip on her own. I didn't want Ryan and Ella to resent their sister and so my husband and I silently endured the financial concerns and did the best we could.

"Well, how was the party? Is Ashley happy she's all done?" I asked trying to shift the conversation to a happier tone.

"It was great. I made a big cake, and Molly Penny was there too. I'm so glad it's over and that we'll never have to go through this again." Kelly told me.

I could hear the relief in her voice. Kelly never ceased to amaze me. She had no doubts whatsoever that Ashley would never suffer a relapse, and that this last six months would only be a bad memory that she would try hard to forget.

Ashley had had her own share of scares during her treatment, and it warmed my heart to know that for Ashley and Kelly, the nightmare was over.

Unfortunately, as time went on, Kelly was to be reminded of

cancer as she ended up losing her Grandmother to the disease not long after, and her own father-in-law was diagnosed with cancer not long after that.

"Great Kel. Promise me you'll remind me to have your optimistic outlook when Colleen is finished her chemo, OK?"

Kelly was a constant source of strength to me as I kept in touch with her over the year. She was always so supportive and positive and told me that Colleen would be fine, that she was a fighter, and that there was nothing to worry about.

"Will you have a party too?"

"Kel, it's so far away, I don't know what we'll do"

Now the day was finally here.

I took the day off and went to the hospital with Colleen. I wanted to know where we went next now that it was all over.

I was told that there would be an "end of treatment" meeting soon where the doctors would talk to us about the "after-care" clinics and the continued monitoring they would do.

Up until this day we still hadn't been told she was in remission, and I was hoping that at this meeting we would get the good news. After her blood tests and immunoglobulin transfusion we headed home to administer her last chemo.

"Did you want to have a party, Colleen?" I asked as I handed her the last pill? It sure felt weird not to give her any more chemo and I knew we had to try to establish a whole new routine.

"No, why?" She asked me not really understanding what I meant.

"It's just that when some kids are finished they have a party to celebrate." I could see by the look on her face that she didn't really want a party and be reminded of the last two years. She was slowly putting all of this behind her and didn't see what she had been through as a reason to celebrate.

As it turned out we did have a celebration for Colleen. On May 24, 2006, it was her one year off-treatment party. We made a sandwich tray and goodies and brought it to the nurses and doctors on one of her routine appointments. She was still receiving the blood transfusions for her immunity and it seemed like a suitable time to acknowledge she was out of the woods for one year.

"Colleen's one year off-treatment," I said to her doctor. "I never imagined this day was even possible. Thank you so much for what you did for her. I'm a believer now and it didn't have to end like it did for my parents or sister."

"It wasn't all "us," Sharon. Colleen had a lot to do with it as well. She's a strong-willed child who doesn't give up. You and Danny should take some credit as well. Not all families deal with things the same way, and in Colleen's case, you managed to find the right balance and attitude."

Chapter Five

END OF TREATMENT MEETING

Early July

It was our end of treatment meeting. We were again taken to a private room where Dr. Mandell, her nurses Deanna and Sue and our social worker Denise sat gathered around a table that was covered with at least 10 thick files of her medical history over the last two years.

This meeting was a lot different in many ways. The professionals who sat before us were not strangers but family to us. They had been there every step of the way and they were as happy about Colleen's success as we were.

Too many times these poor people have had to be with families and support them after their child had died. I could see that they were relieved she had come through the aggressive treatments so well and with very little obvious side effects despite her eye problem and compromised immune system.

Colleen had continued to maintain good spirits and she was enjoying life. She was growing up! She was now in remission and this is not something they can say to everyone. She had finished the race and now the files on the desk were concrete proof about the miracles of modern medicine and how technology can save lives.

Danny and I will always owe an enormous debt of gratitude to these fearless and courageous hard-working people that devote their lives to saving lives and helping families in their time of need. Despite everything, we were given TIME.

And we continue to pray that as the days, and weeks and months turn into years, we would have more TIME to make memories as best we can if you consider the situation.

"The longer she goes without a relapse the better her prognosis," said Dr. Mandell to me looking directly into my eyes. "Research suggests that if the cancer were to return it would likely do so in the next six months," she said trying to sound very professional but I knew she too secretly prayed this wouldn't happen to Colleen.

"After one year that's a real good sign, and by two years, we can say she's definitely got a terrific outlook."

"What about the other children on the clinical trial, how did they all do?" I asked knowing that Colleen's success would help another child somewhere in the world as she was a statistic, but a good statistic, that would spread hope.

"We don't have all the data to share, but Colleen did very well", was all she would say and I could tell from her comment that some of the children had not battled so well.

The doctor then went on to tell us what to expect from now on. She told us honestly that sometimes the side effects of the chemo wouldn't be known for a while and maybe years. There was still a lot more research being done on childhood cancer survivors as they moved into adulthood and no one really knew what to expect.

There was still so much more that needed to be done. Up until recently a lot of children didn't survive so there was very little data on which to draw conclusions. However, with new medicines, research and therapy, the children were living a lot longer and the doctors were busy at work trying to piece it all together and provide answers and identify gaps in the system.

I hoped to myself that maybe in the future they could give us Parents statistics for life expectancy for our children that went beyond the current five-year approach. In our case we had already used up two of these five years in treatment.

She told us some statistics that she did know.

She said there was a chance Colleen could develop cancer in another part of her body that would be a side effect of the chemo and completely unrelated to her original cancer. She said that they would monitor her closely for this eventuality as she would now be part of an "After Care Clinic".

She said that Colleen's situation was a little different from other survivors because she would still need to come to CHEO every month until her immune system didn't need the help of the Immunoglobulins. When her body was functioning on its own, then there would be more time between appointments.

She told us she didn't know how long this would take, and said she may need to receive transfusions for the rest of her life.

We were told that she would mature faster than most children physically, and that if she was still fertile, she should consider not waiting much passed 20 to have children.

She told us that they didn't know if there was going to be

long term neuropsychological damage or how the effects of high dose steroids would manifest themselves in later years. We would just have to "wait and see."

She said that a surgery would need to be scheduled to remove the Port-o-catheter that was still under her skin hooked up to some major arteries. The good news we were given is that her Port-o-catheter had held up the two years. A lot of kids get infections or outgrow the device and must have it removed or replaced. At least Colleen had been spared this extra surgery and complication.

She went on to say a few more things and Danny and I listened intently trying to absorb all the details. At the end of the meeting we thanked them again and instead of heading down the corridor into her room to start the chemo, we headed out to the parking lot and drove home where the kids were waiting to go on summer holidays.

July, 2005, Camp Trillium

I would be lying if I told you that all the worry was over when she stopped taking the chemo and after our end of treatment review. To this day we never stop worrying. Every sniffle, every rash, every cough or ache or pain is cause for panic. Nothing is predictable anymore and we have no idea what the future will be.

I am trying to convince myself that this is actually the way it is with the rest of the world, just that people are too busy to think about it. No one knows what tomorrow will bring, and sometimes we take for granted that things will continue on without too many disruptions.

Every day I wake up in my bed with my husband beside me and the children all in their rooms I tell myself that it will be a good day, because we are all together. I try to keep this attitude as the day unfolds.

I try to stay positive and look for the good. I must confess some days it's hard. And at night, when I tuck my children into bed, then head to bed myself, I try to calm my own mind from worrying about tomorrow so I don't wake up in the night with the same bad dreams based on real events.

Colleen had already used up her wish halfway through treatment, so we didn't have any major trips to look forward to. It was suggested to us that we should go to Camp Trillium.

This is a camp for families of children who have had cancer. We were closest to the Garrett's Island Camp near Picton, Ontario, so I set about making arrangements to go. There was also a camp near Barrie, but that was too far from us here in Ottawa.

It was a terrific experience of which we'd had no idea what to expect. The "Veterans" who go back every year seemed to take a little pleasure watching the "rookies" arrive. Apparently, camp is free every year to the child and their families regardless if they are on treatment, in remission, or passed away.

At the end of the week on the island we had made a lot of friends. The conditions were rustic, but they added to the magic.

A lot of the counselors were siblings of children with cancer, or were cancer survivors themselves. Every day was full of activities for everyone, and a volunteer was assigned to each family so the parents could steal away and have some time for themselves.

We went on a catamaran, used sail boats, went rock climbing, and walked across tightropes. There were nightly campfires and skits, as well as talent shows and hockey games.

I was the only one brave enough to participate in their "swim across the lake tradition" as I am a fairly good swimmer. It took almost an hour to swim across the inlet in Lake Ontario, and I loved every minute of it.

The only thing that was unsettling was the checking in and out of the medicine. Colleen was now off treatment and receiving no formal medication. I remember she did have to take some Polysporin for her eye because one of them had not completely healed since the episode in March with the Pink Eye.

You would have to wait your turn in the lounge of the nurse's station until it was your turn to give your child their medicine. Some of the children there had just started their chemo, so it would take awhile if you got in line behind them.

I was glad that we had not gone to Camp Trillium when she was first diagnosed, because I noticed that a lot of children had to be taken to the nearby Kingston Hospital for blood transfusions and IV therapy as a result of the side effects of their chemo.

Thinking back, we probably would have had the same unfortunate interruption in our stay that may have cast a shadow over our family time and altered our memories of such a wonderful experience.

Fall, 2005

The rest of the summer went the way it usually did for us, except that Colleen's health was very good thanks to the Immunoglobulins, so we tried to enjoy our trailer as much as possible.

By August we were getting ready for going back to school. Colleen was going into Grade 4 and very excited. It was also her Ninth Birthday in September.

One of the Child Life Workers who got along great with Colleen named Brenda, called it her "Champagne Birthday". She was born on the ninth month, the ninth day, and she was actually born at 9:00 a.m. because that is when my C-section was scheduled.

Colleen was again one of Terry Fox's Official team Members for our Community run in mid September, but this year we didn't need any adult strollers. We all ended up doing the 10 kms on our bikes and were closer to finishing first than at the end of the pack like last year.

The memory of our last 2 Christmas's still burned in my mind as the Calendar moved towards December.

Colleen was still going monthly for her transfusions, and her eye was still a constant worry full of infection everyday. Despite these minor nuisances, she was fine, and really excited about the impending Holiday.

We decided to stay home for Christmas because we hadn't been at home as a family on Christmas for over 3 years. We invited my brother and his boys, and my sister from Montreal came too. Her daughter was in Cuba with her new husband and she would have been all alone.

My husband's family understood that we didn't want to make the trip. I was still imagining Colleen getting very sick over the Holiday and didn't want to go too far away from the hospital.

As it turned out she was extremely healthy and we had no worries at all. Everyone had a terrific time, and it even snowed so we could have snowball fights and build snow forts.

As we rang in the year 2006 with our pots and pans on the front porch, I couldn't shake the feeling that there was going to be something go wrong with Colleen's health this year. I didn't know what, when, and how, I just knew "that" something was going to happen.

MARCH BREAK, 2006

"Get in the car guys, it's time to go," I said to Colleen, Ryan, and their cousin Niall who were outside on the driveway. Ella was in Italy on the class trip she had been saving for over the last year, so Danny and I decided to find something for the rest of us to do.

"Mom, I don't want to sit in the middle," said a defiant Ryan to me as I approached the car. "It's Colleen's turn"

"Ryan, we already discussed this. Niall is going to get the window seat first, and then you will have a turn. For now its best if you sit beside Niall so you can link up your Game Boys" I said hoping that I was diffusing his frustration.

Niall had just come in from Toronto yesterday and was joining us for our trip to Myrtle Beach. He is blind having lost his sight to a degenerative eye disease. His sister Roisin also was born with the same condition.

Coincidentally she was also in Italy on a class trip and may actually cross paths with Ella. She and Ella were like sisters to each other, and Roisin had been a good confidant to her while Colleen was so sick.

Despite his blindness, Niall still was very good at video games, he played by sound and touch, and he and Ryan were also good friends.

Colleen had been sick the whole week leading up to the March Break and hadn't been at school. She had been relatively healthy up until Christmas, but after Christmas I noticed she was picking up quite a few illnesses.

We had decided to book this trip a month ago when she was fine because I wanted her to have something to look forward to. It had seemed like a good idea at the time, so I found an amazing deal on the internet for a room that came completely equipped with a kitchenette and overlooked the ocean.

"You feeling OK, honey? Still want to go?" I asked her one last time before getting in the car.

She appeared to be on the mend, but she was still coughing and blowing her nose. Her eye was full of pus and she was having nose bleeds. I couldn't help but remember Christmas 2003 and how familiar this all seemed with her symptoms.

The big difference was that she wasn't on chemo and so her blood counts wouldn't be dropping and making matters worse. If we stayed home, then she would just be sitting on the couch in front of TV for the next few days, and if we left, then she would be sitting in the car.

I thought to myself that if she didn't get better too quickly then sitting on the couch looking over the ocean might be a nice change of scenery. It was up to her though, and I wanted to make sure she felt up to the trip.

"I'm fine. I'm feeling a lot better Mommy. I can't wait to play mini-putt. My friend says that they have the biggest mini-putts in Myrtle Beach!"

And with her blessing and renewed spirits, we left.

It took us two full days to get to our destination. We had to stop every two hours for the kids because they could only sit so long before getting restless.

Danny and I cringed every time one of them asked, "Are we there yet?" After the twentieth time of answering the same question I decided I would never again drive this far with the kids.

It was OK to travel when they were babies, you didn't understand the questions if they had any, and they slept a lot. Now they were real little people, full of questions and complaints, and sometimes the odd squabble.

I couldn't wait to get there myself and relax by the ocean, so I secretly kept asking my husband if we there yet? I had to keep reminding myself that the trip was part of the fun, and at least we were all together experiencing new things.

We finally got there and the room was beautiful and a lot more than we had expected. It was still the off-season and so the rates were very reasonable. We settled in and made plans for the next few days.

"Who wants to go to Ripley's Believe It Or Not Aquarium?" I asked after just putting down one of the flyers I had picked up in the lobby.

"I do," yelled Colleen from the living room. She was still running a little bit of a fever and blowing her nose and having nosebleeds, but she didn't seem any worse to me than when we had left.

I had purchased out of country health insurance and had hoped I wouldn't have to use it. It always seemed like a maze of paperwork to me if you went to the doctor, to get your claims approved.

Years ago when Ella was a baby we had been camping in the States and she developed an infection. It took me nine months to get reimbursed and I'll never forget the hassles.

"Well, we'll plan it for the last day here, that way you'll have more time to get better," I said praying that she would start to kick this bug.

For the rest of the day we swam and took a few strolls on the beach, and watched the sun set over the ocean from our balcony in our room. We all got to bed early and were encouraged by the weather reports that said the next few days were going to be unseasonably warm for Myrtle Beach in early March.

"39.2 degrees" I said to Danny the next morning "That's high and she's had this fever way too long."

"I agree. I can see the rash coming back on her arms and legs. I don't know if it's because she's so pale or if the cancer is coming back." Danny was as terrified as I was and I was starting to think that this whole trip was a big mistake.

I guess I hadn't considered a relapse now, and had pushed the thought out of my mind because I knew that this would be a good break for the family and everyone was looking forward to it. Just goes to show that there are no guarantees and life is full of surprises.

"That's not all, Dan. Do you notice her neck? I'm trying not to be too intrusive so she gets suspicious herself, but can you see the lymph nodes like I do?"

He looked over at Colleen more closely then went over to give her a hug. When he came back to me he said, "I do."

"That's it. I'm taking her to the doctor this morning. I don't want to spoil your day, so why don't you take the boys swimming and play on the beach. There's no need for both of us to waste this gorgeous day by being inside a doctor's office," I said trying to sound brave enough that he would be convinced to do as I asked.

I could see he wanted to come too, but just like when she was first diagnosed, we both didn't need to be there, and one of us had to look after the other kids. "It's early, and maybe we'll get lucky and be home before lunch. I'll call later and let you know if we're going to be later"

I was imagining all sorts of scenarios and my panic attacks started coming at regular intervals. What if the doctor confirmed she had relapsed? Would they call CHEO and would her doctors there tell us to take an emergency flight back? Would we have to be admitted to a cancer hospital in the States? Would the insurance I purchased cover cancer treatments?

If she relapsed would she need to have a bone marrow transplant? I had to take deep breaths and calm myself down. I still had to find a doctor, drive there without getting in an accident, and then prepare myself for the worst. This was not a good time to fall apart. There would be time for that later.

As we waited to be seen by the doctor, I knew I had to say something to Colleen. She was being oddly cooperative and I could see that she was sensing my worry.

"I just want to make sure you're OK Colleen, and then we can go back to enjoying our vacation, and I can take you to Captain Hook mini-putt we passed yesterday." She had been in such awe of all the mini-putts we had passed on the way to the Hotel and everything her friend had told her about how big they were was true.

"OK," was all I got from her. I decided to take it one step further.

"Colleen, there is a very small chance that…well, there is the smallest possibility that…maybe your cancer has come back." I choked back the tears gathering in my eyes as I remembered all of the statistics I had read and the fact that this was a very strong likelihood.

I didn't want her to have to go through all of that again, and I felt powerless to avoid it. Things were just getting back to normal, and the whole routine of hospitals and chemo was not something I was sure she had the strength to endure or me either for that matter.

She looked at me in the eyes and I could tell that she was thinking the same thing. "It's OK, Mommy, don't worry about me."

We were finally called in to see the doctor. After relaying all of her medical history to the nurse I could sense an unspoken judgment forming in her mind. If your child has been so sick, why are you here?

I wanted to say that we would always be facing the unknown

and couldn't live our lives in a bubble; it wasn't fair to her or any of us. We had to move on, and try to live within this reality.

I decided not to enter into a conversation and we waited for the doctor to come into the room.

The doctor examined Colleen and confirmed that her lymph nodes were indeed swollen. He felt her tummy, and her spleen and liver were also enlarged. He also noticed the rash on her skin.

"How long are you staying in Myrtle Beach?" He asked me as he helped Colleen up off the table.

"A couple of more days and then we are heading home." I told him as I struggled to contain my hysteria.

"I want to call an Oncologist colleague of mine and explain what I've found. Give me a minute, I'll be right back." And with that he left Colleen and I alone in the room.

"Colleen, he's going to see if we can stay or have to go home now and to CHEO." I said to her as my heart sank through the floor.

"OK, Mommy," was all she said to me.

When the doctor came back he said that the Oncologist was a little concerned about what he had found. He told him that it sounded a lot like a relapse. He said that we should be fine to finish off our Holiday, but to make it home quickly and call the hospital when we got back to Canada.

What did this mean? Was this some hidden way of telling us to enjoy the last vacation we'll have for a very long time?

Did the fact that she had already had cancer make it less urgent to get treatment?

Was her prognosis so poor now that it really didn't matter when we got back?

In the beginning the doctors were so quick to start things; it seemed as if I was getting the message that things moved a lot differently when the cancer came back.

"Good luck, Mrs. Ruth. Here's a prescription for antibiotics anyway. It's very strong and will be finished by the time you get back to Canada. At least we are doing something, and seeing if the antibiotics help is always the first step." He said to me, and I could tell that he was sincere and saddened by the conversation with the oncologist he'd just had.

I remembered the doctor back in Kemptville who had prescribed the antibiotics before the long weekend in May, 2003.

I went to the drug store and then back to the hotel. Danny and the boys were on the beach and I waved down to them from the balcony.

Colleen was sleepy from the Tylenol and was stretching out on the couch to take a nap.

After feeding the boys lunch and planting them in front of video games while Colleen slept, Danny and I left the room to find a private place to talk where I could tell him what happened.

We ended up going to a little restaurant across the street that sold "crawfish" as their specialty. I had decided that if the doctor said we could finish our Holiday, then that's what we would do. Try to put what had happened earlier in the day out of my mind, and get on with the vacation.

It was easier said than done. Angel Isaac.

"What are you two celebrating?" Asked our waiter as he brought over the menus. Danny and I were holding hands and were leaning into each other across the table as I finished telling him what the doctor had said.

"We're celebrating the relapse of our daughter's cancer." I said completely out of the blue to this total stranger.

He was tall and skinny and was wearing blue jeans. He had a big mane of white hair atop his head, and he didn't look like he was American or belonged in Myrtle Beach.

"Oh, I'm so sorry." His name was Isaac. I learned that he was not from the US, but he never told us where. He said he was just passing through and was working to make a few extra dollars so he could continue his trip.

"This may be the last time my husband and I can go out together for such a long time." I said remembering how Danny and I were two ships that passed in the night when she was originally diagnosed.

I was also worried that we would be separated for a long time if she would have to have a bone marrow transplant. This was considered salvage therapy at relapse for her type of cancer.

They usually only did these in Toronto Sick Kids. One of us would need to be with her and one of us at home with the other kids.

We stayed for our food to arrive, but neither of us was very hungry. We boxed up our meals, paid the bill, and headed for the door to go back to the room and check on the kids.

He came out of nowhere. After he took our order we hadn't seen him again. Someone else had brought our food and taken our money. "Hold on" he said as he came up to us. "I don't normally do this," he said as he placed one hand on my shoulder and one hand on Danny's, "But can I pray for your daughter? What's her name?"

We were taken completely off guard by him, but both Danny and I felt the same way about people who wanted to pray for Colleen. It couldn't hurt. So many people have said prayers over the last three years for her to get better, and I think they worked and God listened. She was a miracle and had overcome so much.

As I think back, a lot of people might feel awkward, but everything was perfectly natural.

We told him her name and he closed his eyes for just a moment his hands still resting on our shoulders.

"Everything's going to be fine," he said to us, "the power of prayer is very strong. I belong to a group that believes strongly in this. I'll ask them to pray for Colleen as well." At that moment I wished that I had left him a bigger tip!

In the room the boys were still playing video games and Colleen was starting to wake from her nap on the couch. I looked down at her and she looked so weak and sick. I hadn't brushed off what had happened in the restaurant with Isaac, I was just feeling so defeated that I couldn't believe what he said would come true.

The rest of the evening was peaceful and between Colleen's nosebleeds we watched the sun set again over the ocean from the balcony in our room and watched a good movie on the TV.

The next morning I went in to check on Colleen. I hadn't given Tylenol yet and I wanted to know what her fever was today to gauge how much activity she could endure.

I was quite surprised to find she had no fever. I was equally surprised to see that the Lymph nodes on the side of her neck were no longer visible to the naked eye.

I couldn't see any signs of the rash. She was also talkative and had more energy than in a long time. She had only had one dose of the antibiotics by now, was it possible that they worked so fast?

As the question formed in my mind I knew that the antibiotics were not the reason why overnight she seemed to get better. It was Isaac. Angel Isaac. We were witnessing a miracle and if I ever had any doubts that angels walked the earth, I didn't now.

"It's a miracle, Danny." I said as I went back into our room to tell him how Colleen was.

He agreed when he went in to see her. I know that as I write this there will always be people who don't believe in miracles, or angels, or the power of prayer, but we have witnessed first hand what happened.

There is no doubt in my mind that if we hadn't run into Isaac, and he hadn't have said his prayer, that things may have turned out a lot differently.

At Colleen's insistence we went to the mini-putt later on in the morning, and spent the afternoon playing in the sand on the beach.

The next day she got stronger and so we decided to go to the Ripley's Aquarium. The day after that, we headed home. No more nosebleeds, no more fever, and no more rashes reappeared on our trip.

When we got back home I called the hospital and explained what had happened. Because Colleen didn't appear sick now, and was running no fever, they told us to wait to bring her in until her next appointment in a few days.

The "after-care" clinic doctor examined her and said she could still feel a little swelling in the lymph nodes but that she felt no swelling in her belly.

She said she saw a little bit of a lacy rash under her skin, and we agreed to keep an eye on it. Her counts were good and it looked like her immune system was starting to kick in so they were going to start decreasing the dosage of her transfusions and "wait and see" how her body reacted.

Her eye was still having a puss discharge, and an appointment was made for the ophthalmologist. Considering all of the things that could have gone wrong with Colleen over the years, this was a small price to pay for her.

August, 2006

I was just cleaning up the last of the garbage from the party when Colleen came barging into the kitchen. Danny had started a new job and I knew that we wouldn't be getting any vacation time this summer.

I still took my vacation days as I had promised Colleen that she could have her tenth birthday in the summer and not September. She had it in her head she wanted a pool party sleep over. My parks and rec days as a camp counselor came in handy as I planned activity after activity for the eight girls that slept over. It was a 24-hour party and I was exhausted.

"Can Brittany come to the trailer with us?" She asked as I started to fill up the sink with more water to wash the endless pile of dishes.

(After what happened in Myrtle Beach, Colleen's health progressively got better. There were the odd flu's here and there, but nothing compared to what we had gone through.)

I agreed that her friend could come and then turned my thoughts to what I needed to pack for our weekend away.

By the end of August we had bought all our back to school supplies and it was time to go back to the hospital for her regular monthly transfusion and check up.

"The doctor says this is her last transfusion. Her immune system is almost back to normal according to her counts, and she wants to see if Colleen can overcome things on her own without the help of the Immunoglobulins. Her dosage is so small now it's really not worth continuing." Said the nurse to me while we were waiting for our check-up.

I thought about what she said and realized again that we followed the "wait and see approach." I would forever need to find patience with this reality because I'm more of a proactive than a reactive person.

For a moment I got cynical and thought to myself that what they really wanted to see was how sick she got without the immunoglobulins. I quickly tried to dismiss this as being too negative.

The doctors were here to help her get better and make sure her body started to function on its own. How would we know if we didn't try?

I agreed that it was a good approach. During her check-up we got the all clear and were also told that now we didn't have to come back for three months.

School started and things went well.

In Mid September we went to a sports complex in Montreal. Colleen had been invited by Dr. Mandell, her oncologist, to join a few other cancer survivors and take a chance to see if they could soar high in the air on a trapeze.

Dr. Mandell later told me that watching the kids on the trapeze was very special to her. She said that the kids had had to put up with so much they couldn't control, but now they could show they had to power to control what they were doing and take a step off the ledge and soar high above the crowd.

Colleen didn't quite make the back flip on the trapeze bar, but she held on tight and flew back and forth way above our heads. When the kids had all had enough, there was still time left and the parents and siblings were asked if they wanted to try.

Ryan and I wasted no time in signing up for a turn. Danny declined saying that he was probably too heavy and was afraid he would break the equipment. I secretly knew he was afraid of heights. Ella tried to use the same story, so they watched as Ryan and I strapped on the gear and had a blast on the trapeze.

September rolled into October and so far she's been well. I finally got a surgery scheduled for my foot to repair some damage that if left untreated could render me crippled in coming years. I am only 40 and have a lot longer to need my feet. It has been with my recuperation time that I have finally had a chance to finish this story.

It's almost 4:30 p.m. and the kids will be coming home on the bus. I will be going back to work soon as my cast comes off tomorrow, November 14th. This is where the story ends and as you can see we have a happy ending.

Tomorrow starts a new beginning and a new story, and God-willing, happy endings. We'll just have to do what we have come to do best: **"wait and see"**.

A NOTE FROM THE AUTHOR

I have shared with you our own personal journey over the last three years and tried my best to remember dates and times. I tried to relay information to the reader while at the same time tell a story that would keep your attention. All of the events happened and I have changed some of the names of the people to respect their privacy.

As I was writing this book my husband marveled at the things I was able to recall. He has started to block things out and the more time that passes, is getting on with his life. I too feel the memory fading as time goes on and am glad I was able to remember what I did.

I will be forever changed by what happened, and maybe some day, will pick up this book and marvel at the strength, courage and endurance my whole family had to stay together no matter what happened and make the best of a very bad situation.

My other children are happy and also do not want to be reminded of the past. They will be forever changed from what happened to their sister, and I wonder if they'll ever tell me one day of how they felt during everything.

They have both continued to thrive and do well in school. Ryan is still playing hockey, and Ella was chosen to go on a mission trip with her school to Cuernavaca, Mexico, next March Break, 2007.

Colleen is now in french immersion in Grade 5 and she loves it. She's doing just as well as her brother and sister did when they started in Grade 5. She has lots of friends and is maturing into a beautiful young lady.

Her hair is thick and curly and she takes extra effort each morning to make sure she has it just the right way. She doesn't like to be reminded of what happened to her, and seems to want to be known as "Colleen" not "Colleen who had cancer."

She has been very patient with me as I have been writing this book and I can tell that she is glad that I'm finally writing it. She's a very intuitive child who has a lot of compassion and wisdom and knows that maybe somehow this book will help someone.

Everyday I thank God and the Angels who work in the hospital for saving her life. I am glad she was a Guinea Kid and am grateful that she had the chance to participate in that clinical trial.

Thinking back to all of the things that might have happened, and looking at a perfectly normal healthy ten year old is a miracle. She is a miracle of modern medicine.

Never take anything for granted, one day it could be gone. Make the most of each day, and squeeze the life out of each moment. Have the courage to laugh at your mistakes, and always hug the ones you love. Tomorrow will always come, today will pass, and yesterday will fade.

AFTERWORD

THE BATTLE FOR "COMPASSIONATE CARE"

The following pages tell a little different story about a battle that was being fought during the time Colleen was battling cancer. Now that you've had a chance to connect dates and events, I'm sure you'll find the rest of the story very interesting.

I have pieced together some of the articles and emails and support I have had to try to get amendments to the Compassionate Care Bill introduced in January, 2004. Remember the first Christmas you read about in my book in 2003?

I think Colleen was supposed to pull through and I was supposed to write this book. Maybe it will help; maybe it will collect dust on a shelf or be buried in a box in Parliament Hill along with my petition.

She is living proof that there are gaps in our social system and our support systems need to be updated.

Unfortunately to this point I can't say there is a happy ending to this battle. I wish I could, but some battles take longer than others, and sometimes it's hard to tell who the enemy is so it's hard to know how to win.

I have met a lot of people over the last three years who have had the power to effect change. Things just got in the way I guess. I don't blame them. There's always hoping.

A wise lady told me "Sharon, it's such a political onion that needs to be peeled layer by layer". Unfortunately she's right. medicine and politics don't mix.

Compassion and politics and medicine can blow up in your face. How many more families must be made to suffer until the last layer is off?

Compassionate fight hits the Hill
Mom's petition to change benefit requirements in the Commons today

By NELLY ELAYOUBI
Ottawa Sun

OXFORD STATION
Woman presses for more compassionate leave

Fed plan little help for sick girl's kin

By DONNA CASEY
Ottawa Sun

AN OXFORD Station mother whose seven-year-old daughter is fighting late-stage cancer says the government's new compassionate benefit doesn't go families cope

Compassionate Care petition presented
By Louise Mortimer
Advance Staff Reporter

Compassionate Care Benefit petition gets national support
By Louise Mortimer
Advance Staff Reporter

MP's help out with Compassionate Care
By Louise Mortimer
Advance Staff Reporter
Sharon Ruth, the petitioner for

Caregivers to ill, dying to get more EI

Local mother's battle to change bill draws to a close

If you must be absent from work to care for a dying family member, maybe we can help.

Employment Insurance Compassionate Care Benefit

The Government of Canada is introducing Compassionate Care, a new special Benefit available to Employment Insurance eligible workers who must be absent from work to provide support to a family member who is gravely ill with a serious risk of death.

Important facts:
- Beginning January 4th, 2004 six weeks of Compassionate Care Benefits will be available to those who are eligible and provide the required medical certificate.
- The Benefit can be used by one individual or shared and provide family members to care for a child, parent, spouse or common-law partner who is gravely ill with a serious risk of death.

For more information about the Compassionate Care Benefit, call 1 800 O-Canada (1 800 622-6232), 1 800 465-7735 (TTY) or visit www.canada.gc.ca

Government of Canada Gouvernement du Canada

Canada

Mother says EI's compassion is too narrowly focused

Because her daughter may beat her life-threatening illness, the caregiver's benefit does not apply, **NORMA GREENAWAY** reports.